Adelita

Romantic Pieces for Classical Guitar

Compiled and edited by
Dmitrijs Volkovs

The collection includes works by composers and guitarists of the Romantic era, ranging from very simple pieces by Matteo Carcassi to intermediate pieces by Tárrega and Arcas. In addition to widely known pieces played by almost all classical guitar learners, the collection also contains some lesser-known works. The main composers for classical guitar of this period are represented. Alongside those already mentioned, the collection features Spanish guitarist and composer Fernando Sor, Austrian guitarist Josef Mertz, Spaniards José Ferrer and Pascual Roch, and French virtuoso Napoléon Coste.

Copyright © 2024 Dmitrijs Volkovs

ISBN: 978-176382-2399

CONTENTS

1 Romantic Era Composers

4 Allegretto *(Matteo Carcassi)*
6 Allegretto *(Matteo Carcassi)*
8 ANDANTINO *(Mateo Carcassi)*
10 Pastoral *(Matteo Carcassi)*
12 Study in A minor *(Matteo Carcassi)*
16 Etude No.3 Op.60 *(Matteo Carcassi)*
18 Etude No.16 Op.60 *(Matteo Carcassi)*
20 Etude *(Francisco Tarrega)*
22 Lagrima *(Francisco Tarrega)*
24 Etude No.1 *(Francisco Tarrega)*
26 Adelita *(Francisco Tarrega)*
27 Estudio *(Francisco Tarrega)*
29 Etude *(Francisco Tarrega)*
30 Etude in G *(Francisco Tárrega)*
31 Ländler *(Johann Kaspar Mertz)*
33 Romance *(Johann Kaspar Mertz)*
35 Nocturne *(Johann Kaspar Mertz)*
37 Polonaise No.6, Op.13 *(Johann Kaspar Mertz)*
40 Ejercicio *(Jose Ferrer)*
42 EL Amable *(José Ferrer)*
44 Tango n°3 op.50 *(Jose Ferrer)*
46 Tango No.1 *(Julian Arcas)*
48 Bolero *(Julian Arcas)*
51 Tango No.4 *(Julián Arcas)*
52 Habanera *(Pascual Roch)*
54 Valse *(Pascual Roch)*
56 Etude n°14 op.35 *(Fernando Sor)*
58 Pasa-Calle *(José Viñas)*
60 Polka *(José Viñas)*
62 Vals *(José Viñas)*
64 Waltz *(Napoleon Coste)*
67 I lost my Eurydice *(Arr. Napoléon Coste)*
69 Barcarolle *(Napoleon Coste)*
70 Etude No.13 *(Napoleon Coste)*

The era of Romanticism builds upon classical traditions. The 19th century, often referred to as the Romantic century, was also marked by the Industrial Revolution, which brought about significant social tensions, and numerous wars driven by burgeoning nationalism.

In the realm of music, Romanticism is characterized by a strong emphasis on emotion, unbridled virtuosity, and a desire to transcend conventional boundaries. Niccolò Paganini, an Italian violinist who was also a virtuoso guitarist, epitomized Romanticism through the egomania attributed to him and the cult of genius he inspired among virtuosos.

The Spanish guitar maker Antonio Torres, in collaboration with Francisco Tárrega, developed a larger form of the guitar in the late 19th century that remains standard today. Romantic music often features increased use of chromaticism and folkloric elements, coupled with a heightened awareness of tones that capture attention. This is exemplified by Jose Ferrer's tango, which hints at these characteristics. Meanwhile, the simpler compositions by other composers of this chapter, such as Matteo Carcassi and Napoléon Coste, remain firmly rooted in classical music tradition, in contrast to their more complex concert works.

Romantic Era Composers

Matteo Carcassi (1792-1853)

Matteo Carcassi was a famous Italian guitarist and composer. Carcassi began with the piano, but learned guitar when still a child. He quickly gained a reputation as a virtuoso concert guitarist. Carcassi wrote a method for guitar (op. 59) that remains valuable, relevant and interesting, blending technical skills and brilliant romantic music.

Johann Kaspar Mertz (1806-1856)

János Gáspár Mertz was born in Pozsony, Kingdom of Hungary, now Bratislava (Slovakia). A virtuoso, he established a solid reputation as a performer. Mertz's guitar music, followed the pianistic models of Chopin, Mendelssohn, Schubert and Schumann, rather than the classical models of Mozart and Haydn (as did Sor and Aguado), or the bel canto style of Rossini (as did Giuliani).

Napoleon Coste (1805 – 1883)

Napoleon is french and is a major figure in guitar composition of the mid-nineteenth century. Napoleon was taught by his mother at a very early age. Napoleon later became Fernando Sor's student and quickly established himself as the leading French virtuoso guitarist. Napoleon is the first composer to transcribe guitar music of the 17th century to the modern era.

Francisco Tarrega (1852-1909)

Tárrega is considered to have laid the foundations for 20th century classical guitar and for increasing interest in the guitar as a recital instrument. Tárrega preferred small intimate performances over the concert stage. Some believe this was because he played without the nails needed for volume. Others say this was related to his childhood trauma.

José Ferrer (1835-1916)

José Ferrer was a Spanish guitarist and composer, born in Spain. Ferrer studied guitar with his father, a guitarist and collector of sheet music, before continuing his studies with José Brocá. In 1882, he left Spain for Paris in order to teach at the Institut Rudy and at the Académie Internationale de Musique.

Julián Arcas (1832-1882)

Julián Arcas was a Spanish classical guitarist and composer, who influenced Francisco Tárrega and Antonio de Torres. He was "one of the most important figures in Spanish music in the 19th century".

Jose Vinas Y Diaz (1823-1888)

Like many of the Spanish top-guitarists of the mid-19th century, his name was overshadowed by Farncisco Tarrega. Nevertheless, Vinas belongs to the group of compser-guitarsts as Jose Broca, Jose Ferrer, Julian Arcas, Juan Parga, Antionio Cano and Jose Costa.

Allegretto

Matteo Carcassi (1796-1853)

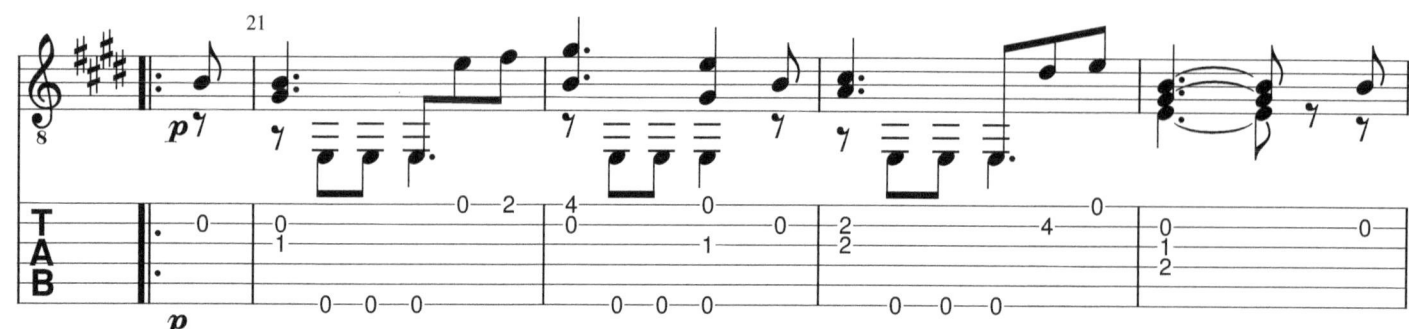
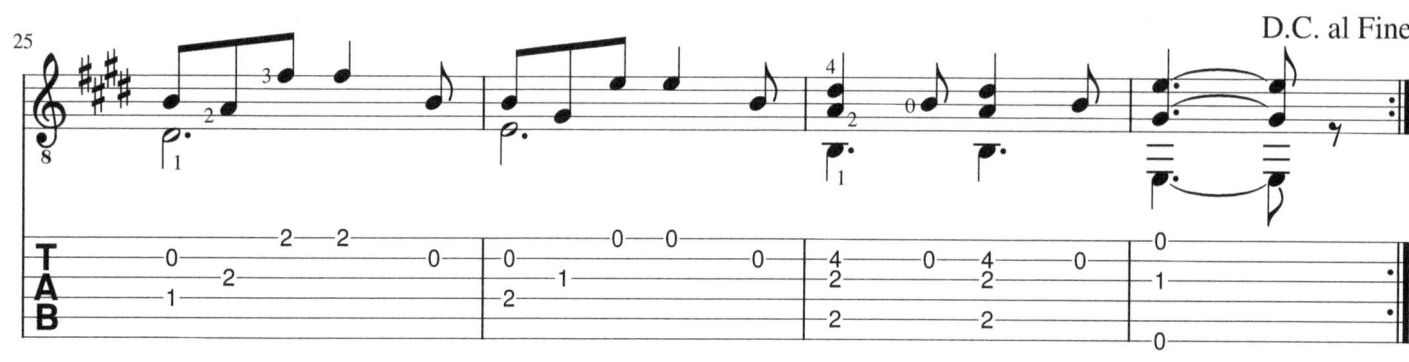

Allegretto

Matteo Carcassi (1796-1853)

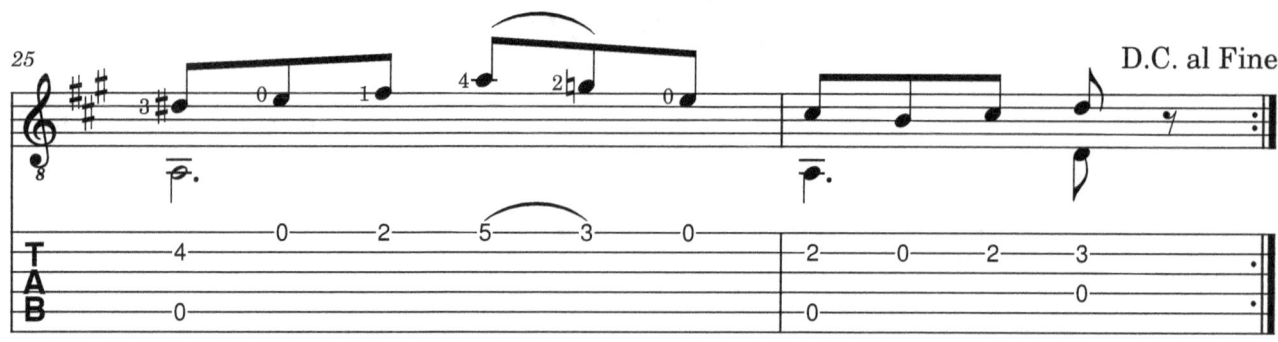

ANDANTINO

Mateo Carcassi (1796-1853)

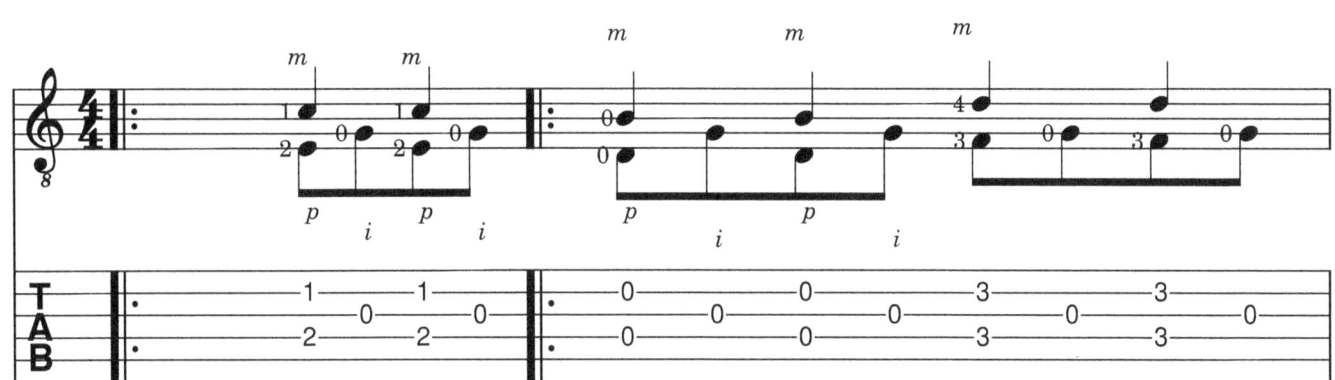
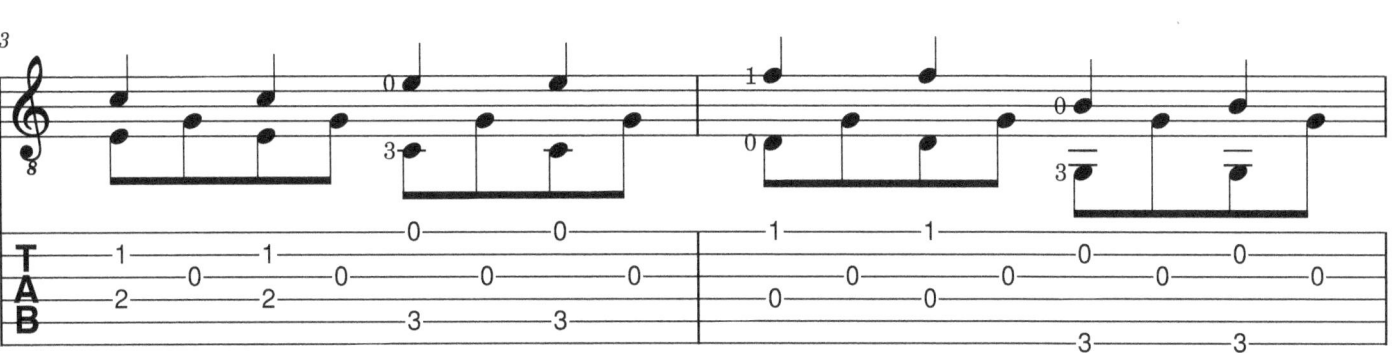
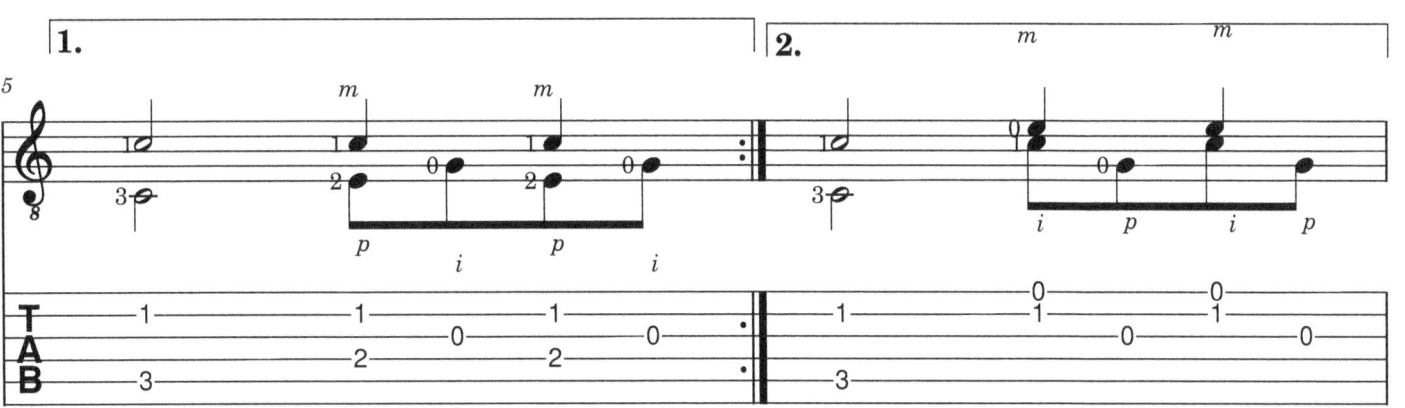
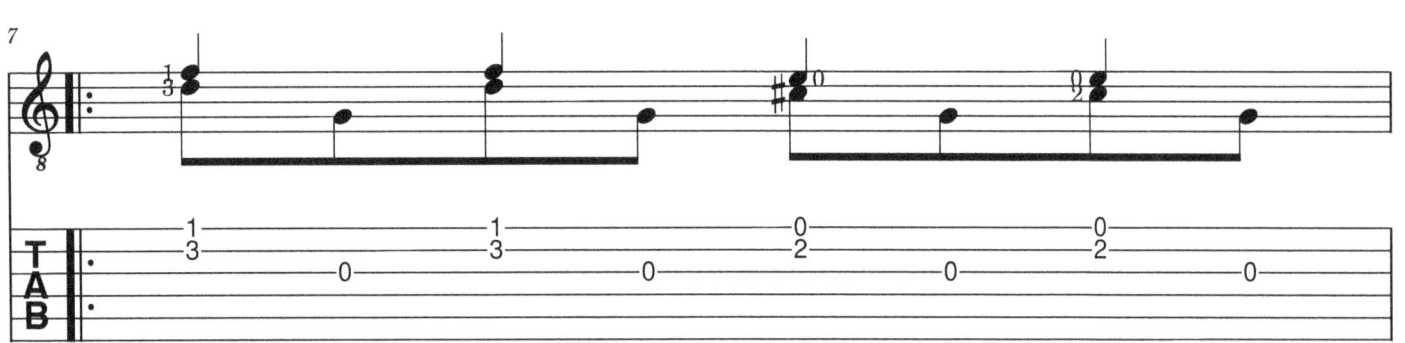

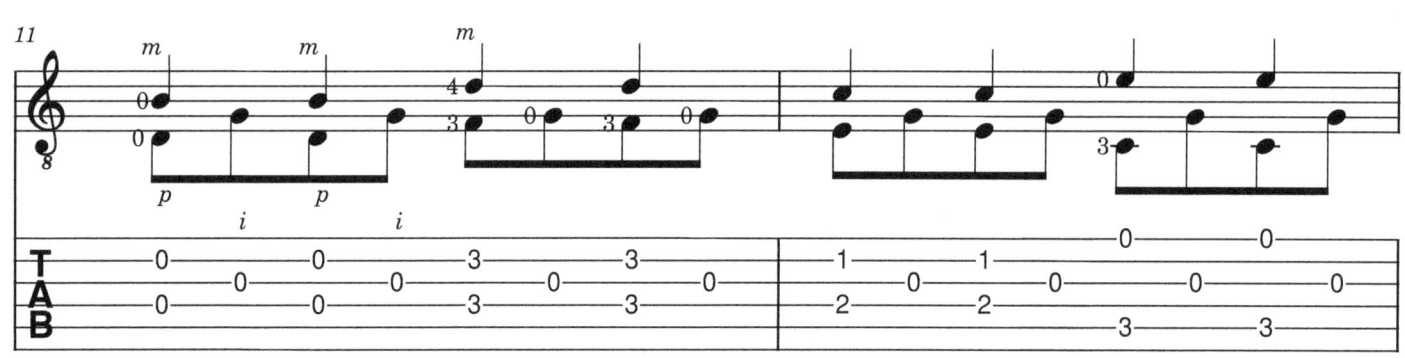
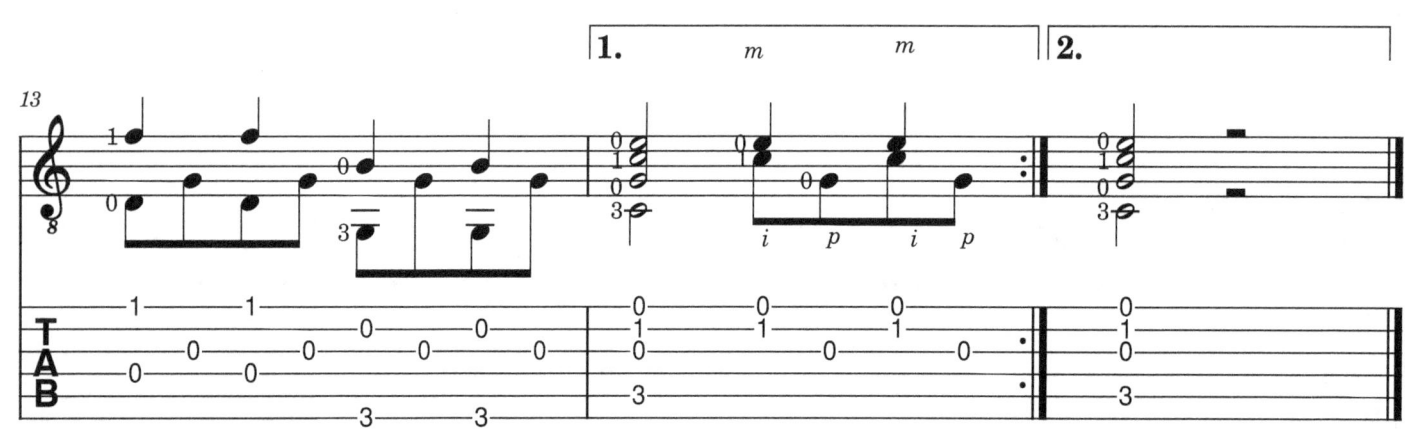

Pastoral

Matteo Carcassi (1796-1853)

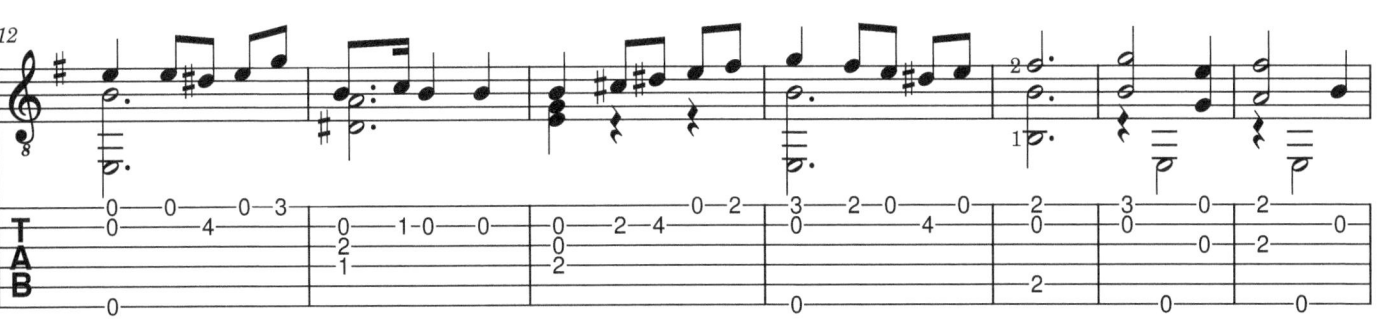

Study in A minor

Matteo Carcassi (1796 - 1853)

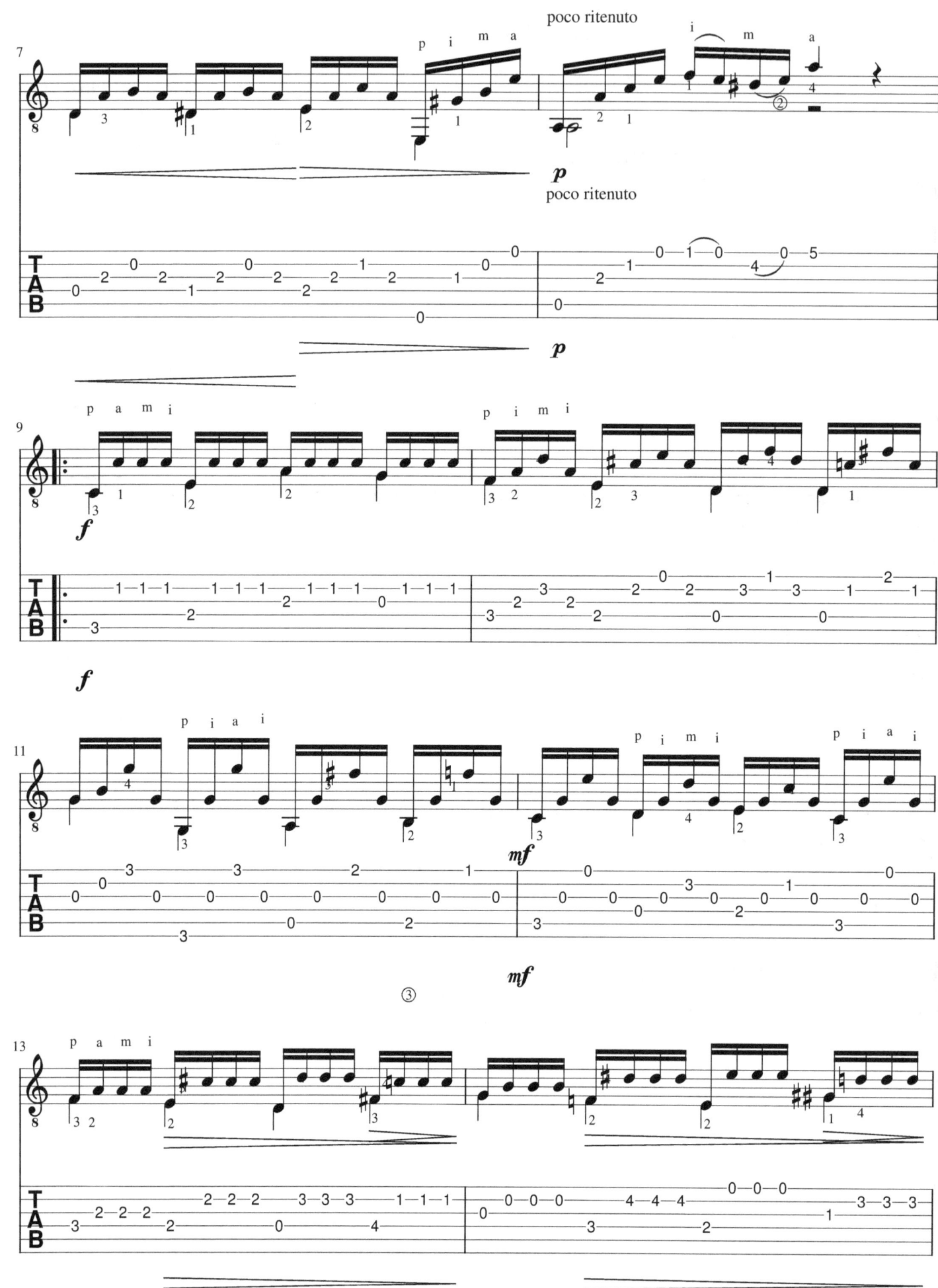

Etude No.3 Op.60

Andantino

Matteo Carcassi (1796-1853)

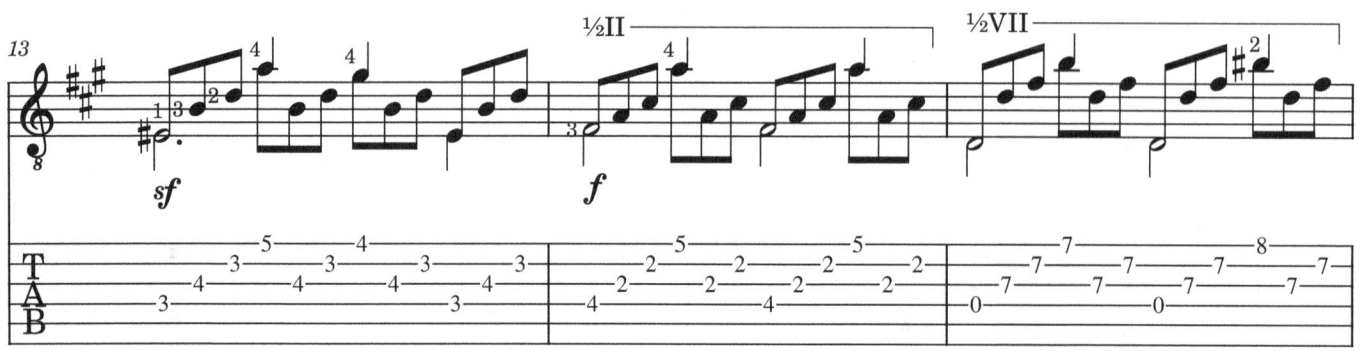
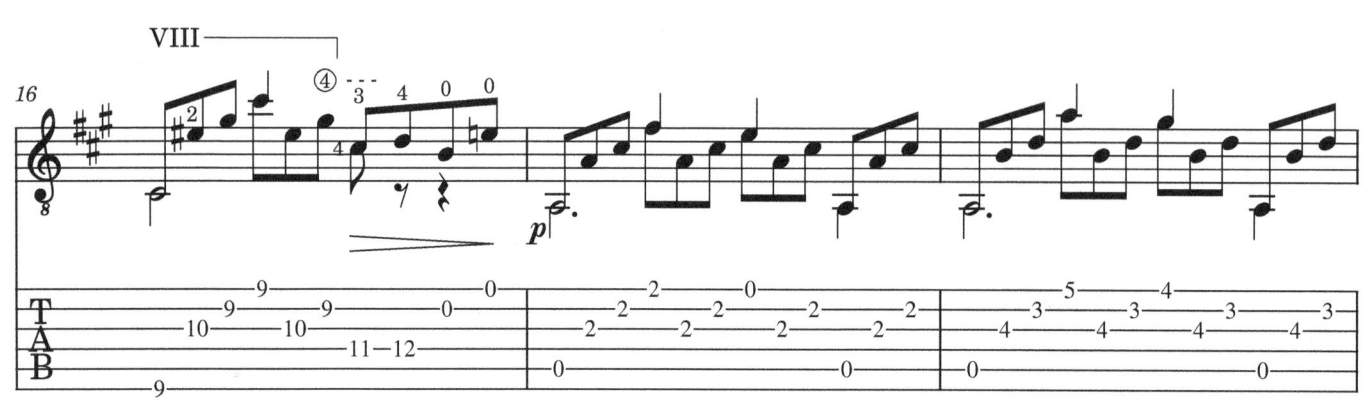
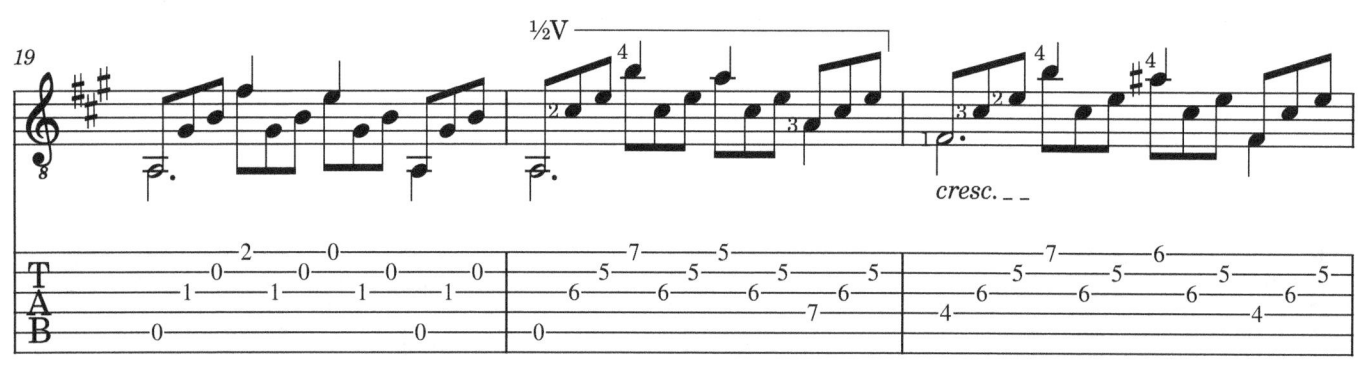
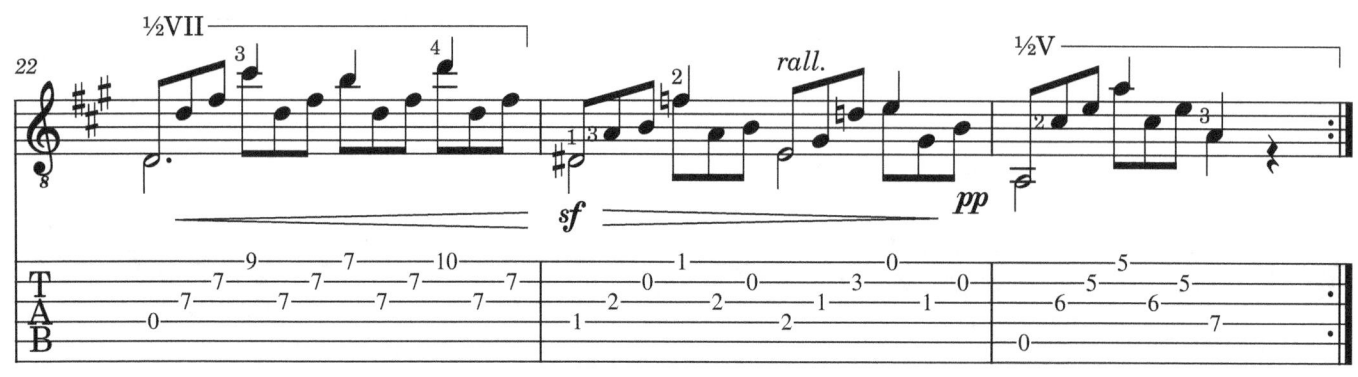

Etude No.16 Op.60

Matteo Carcassi (1792 -1853)

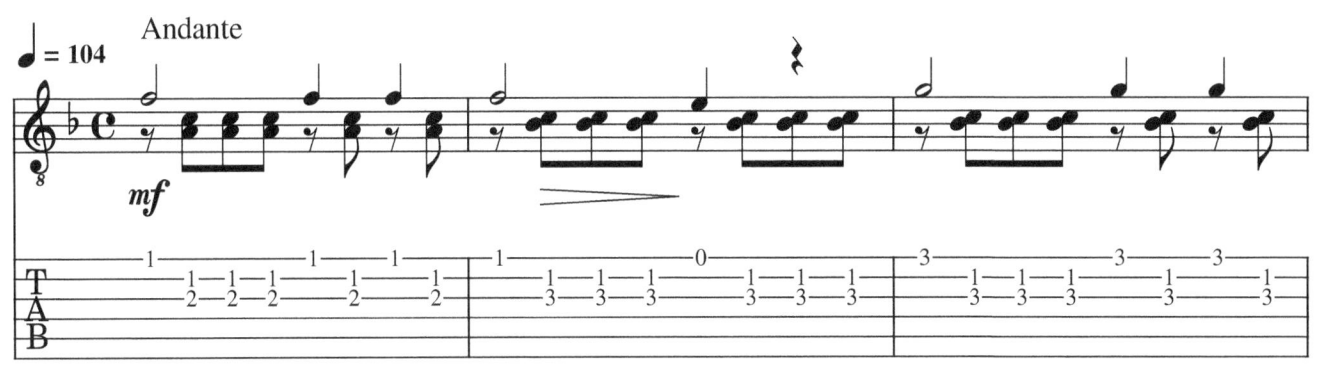
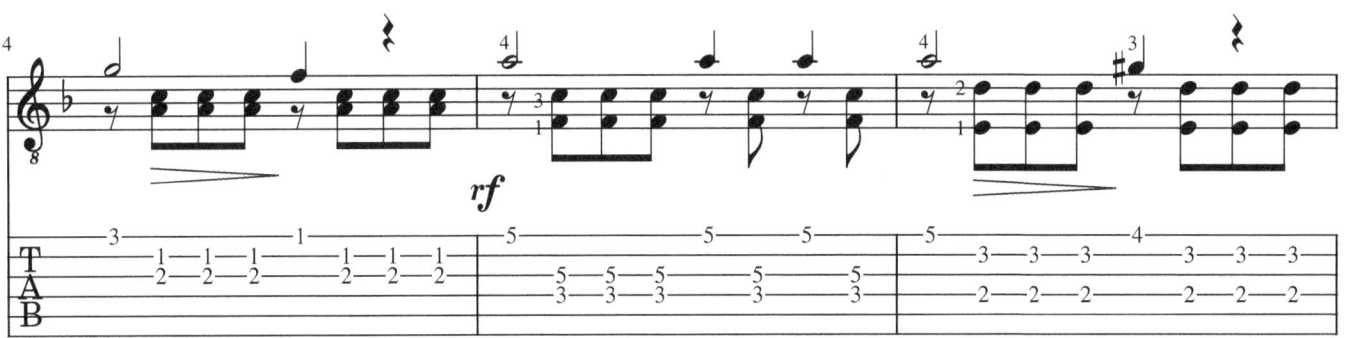
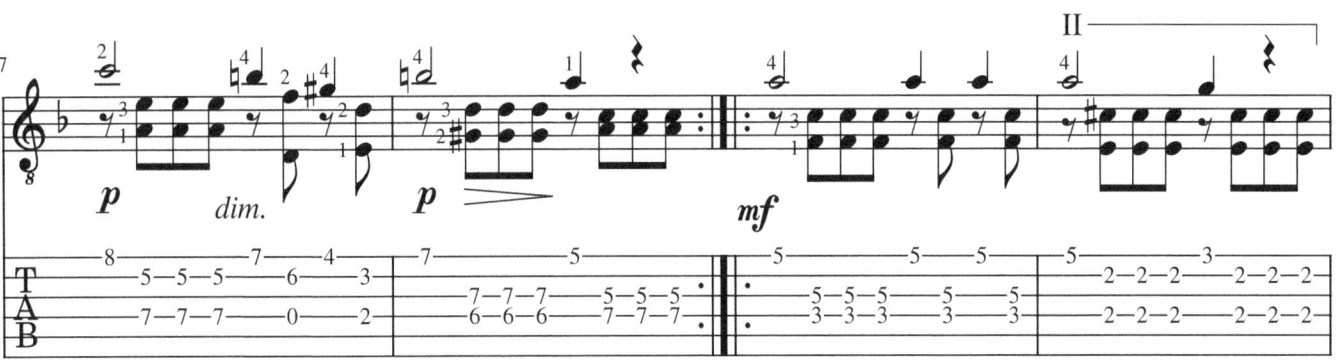

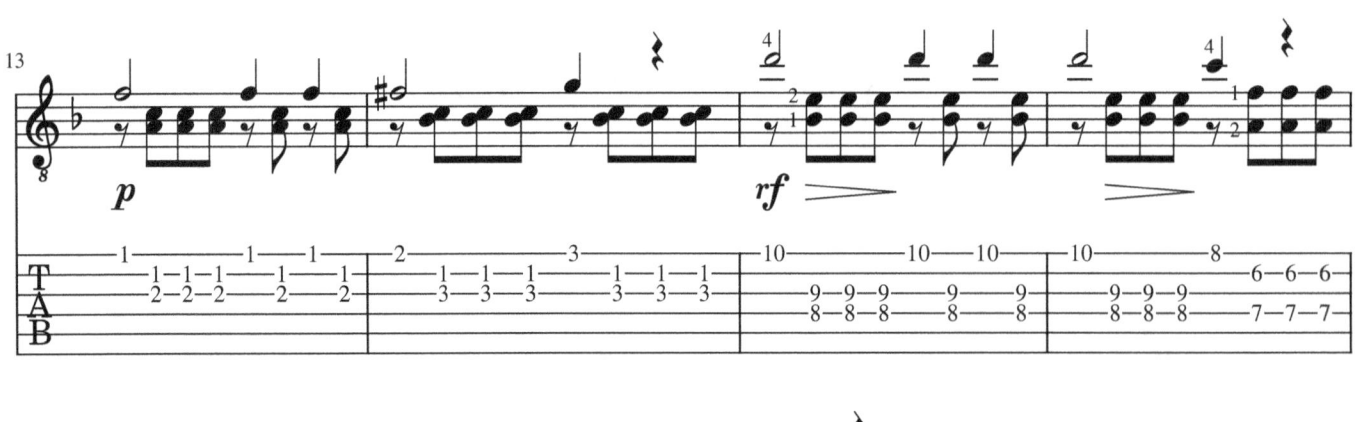
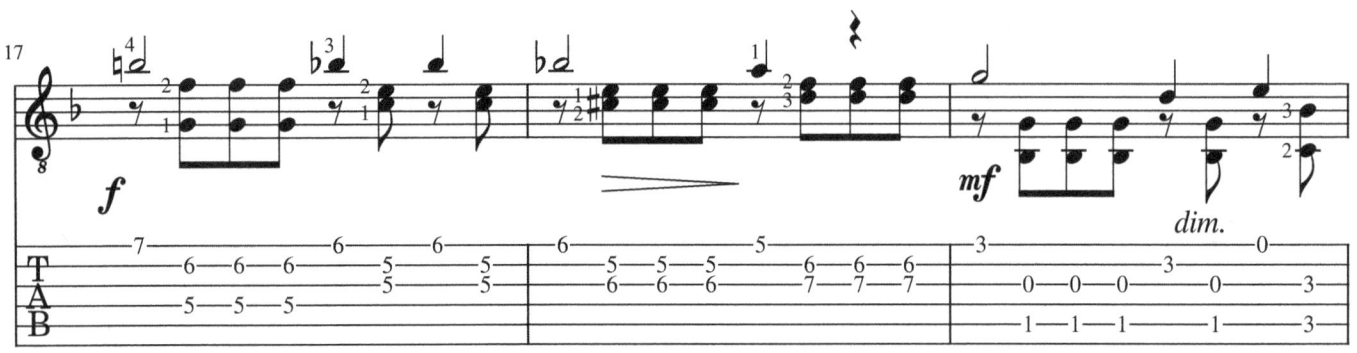
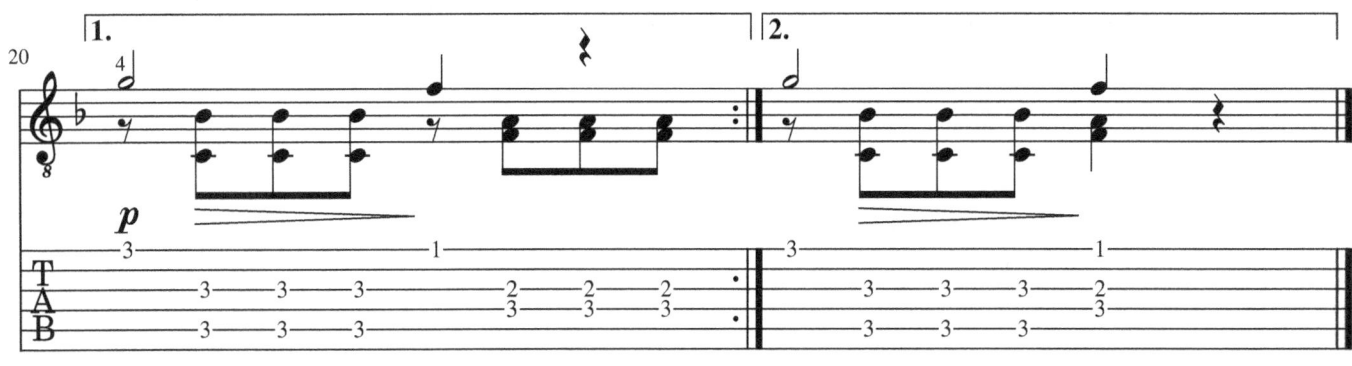

Etude

Francisco Tarrega (1852-1909)

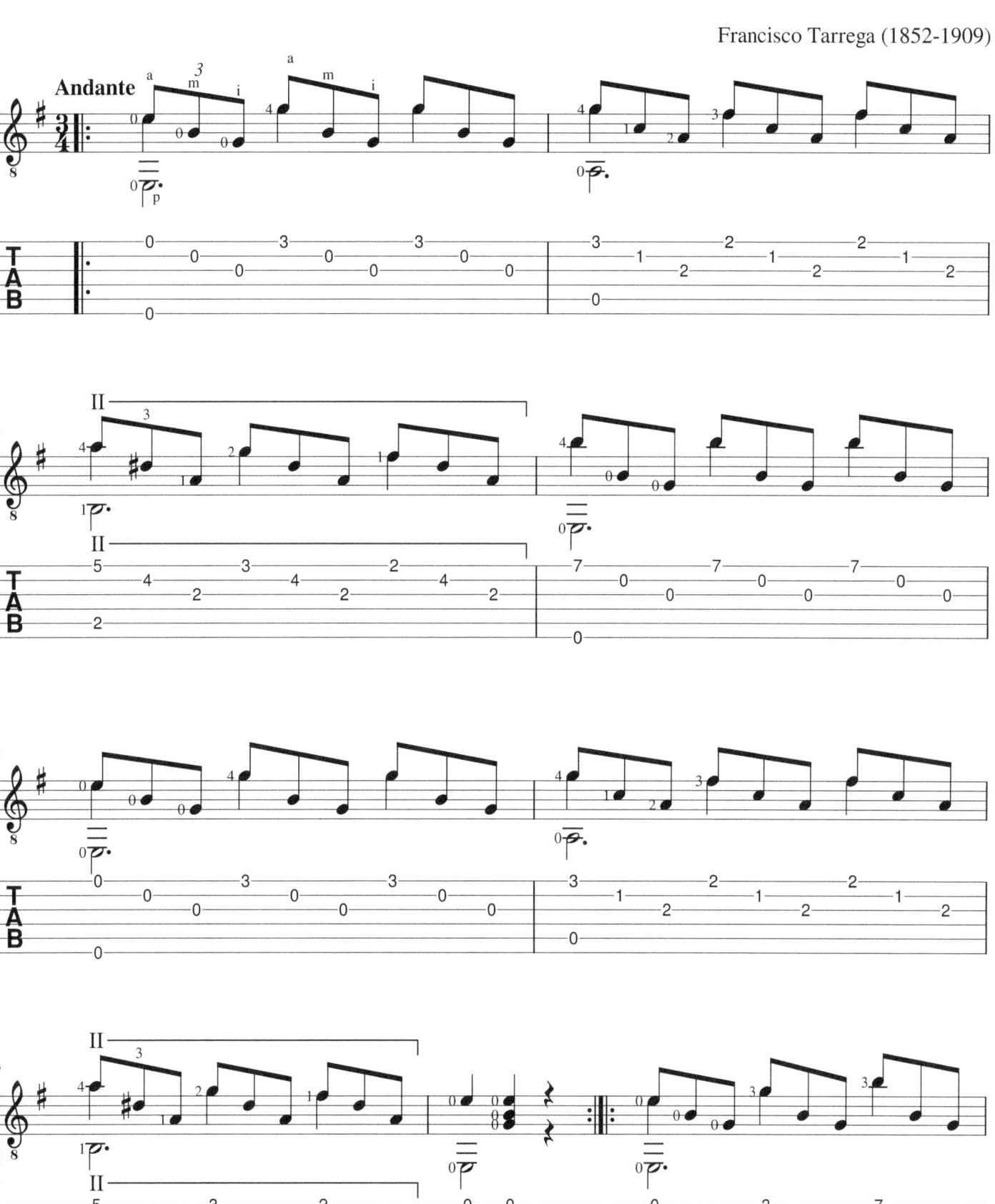

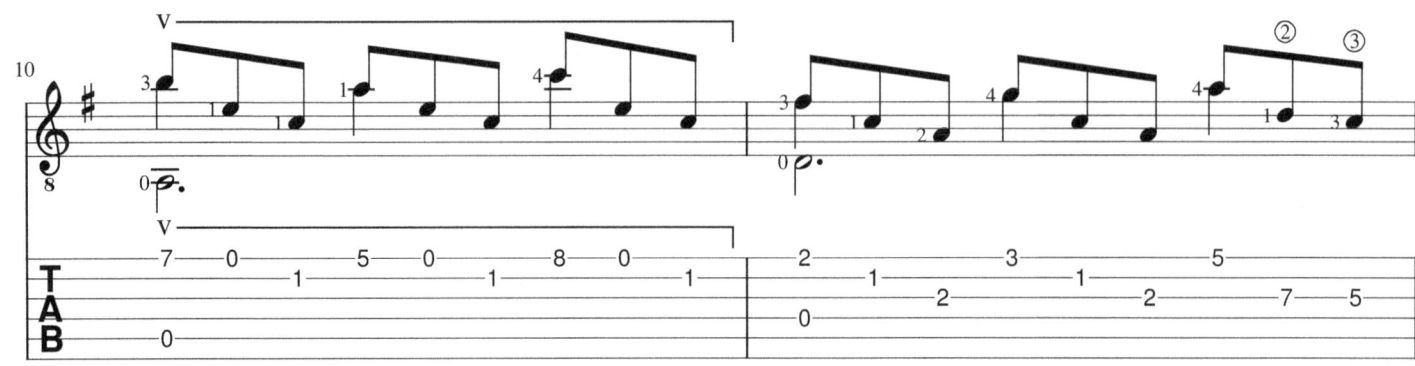
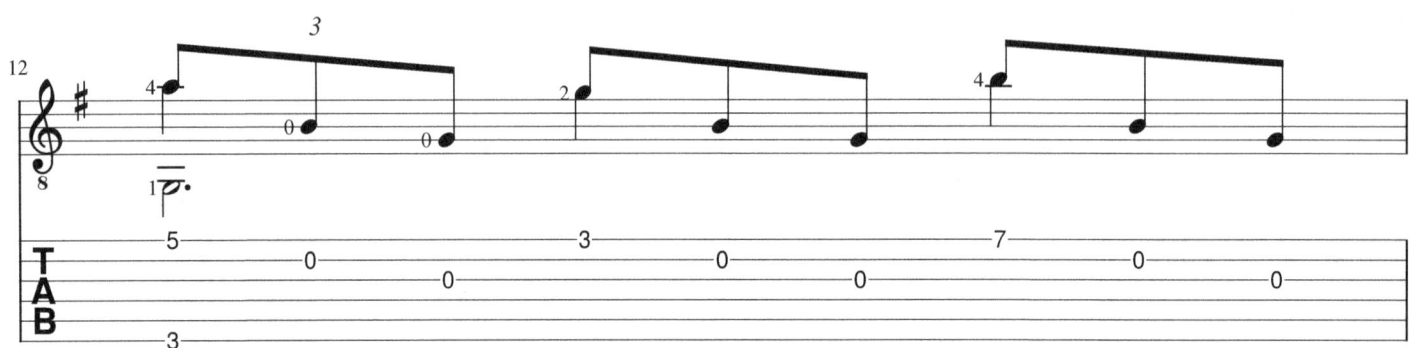
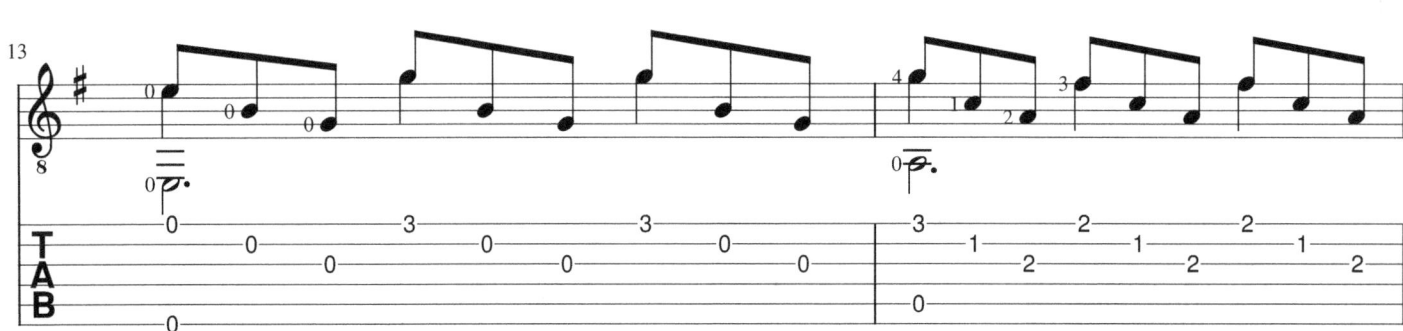
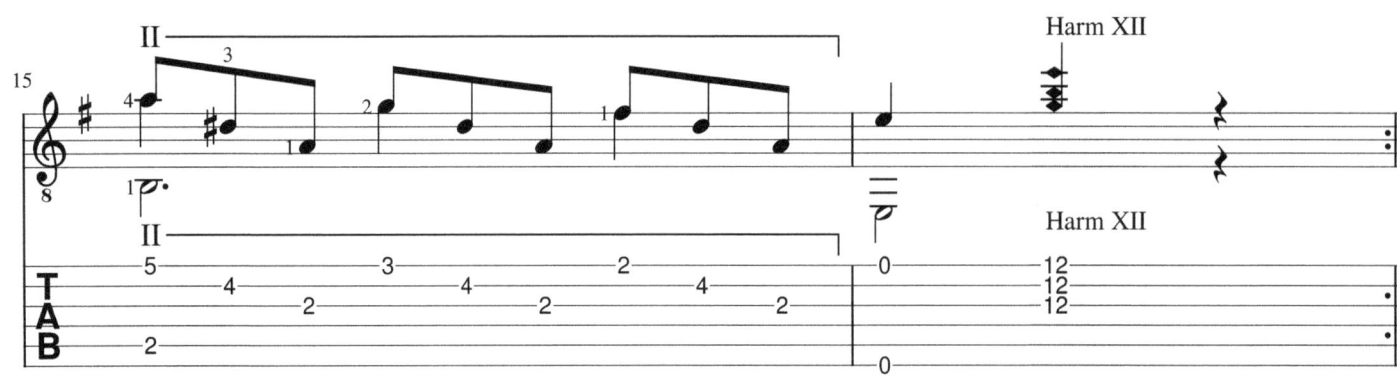

Lagrima

Francisco Tarrega (1852-1909)

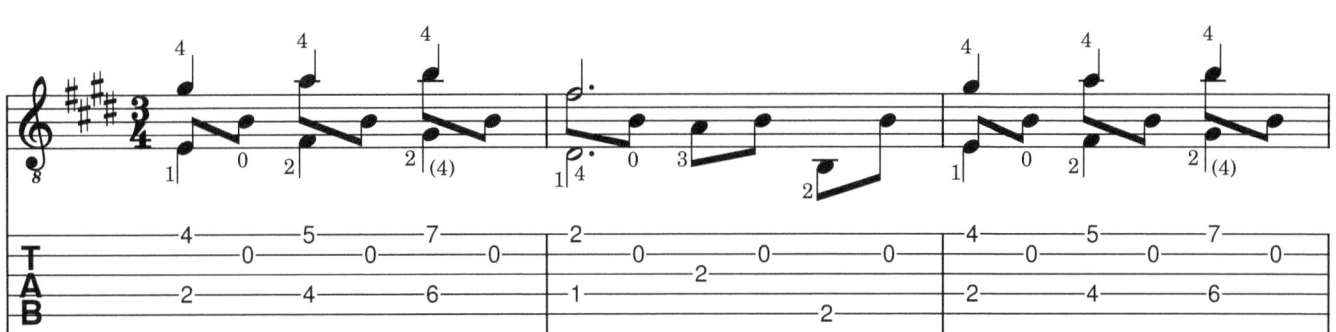
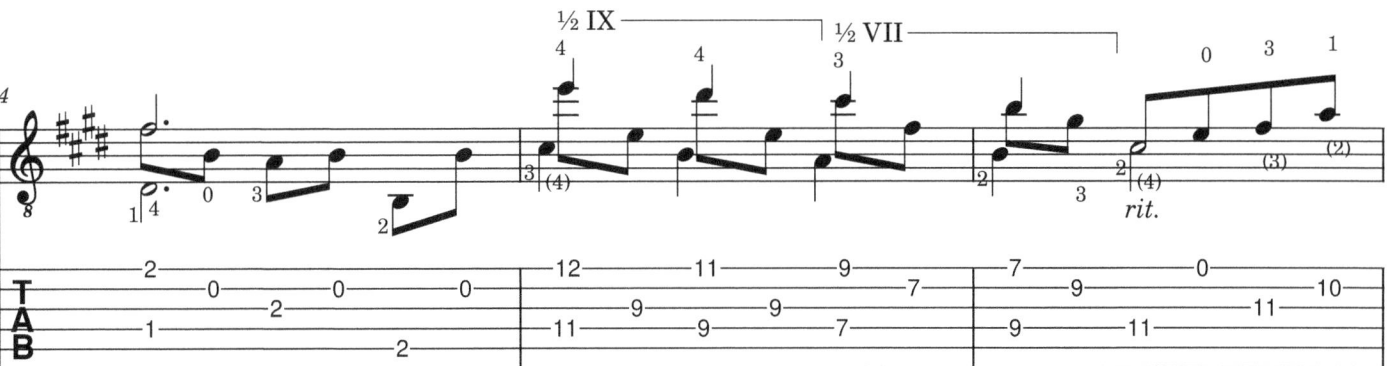
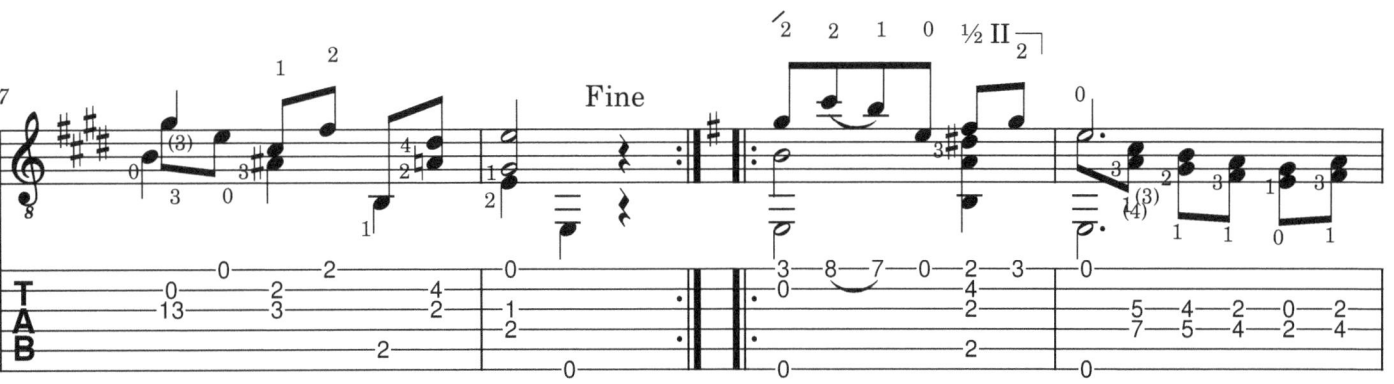

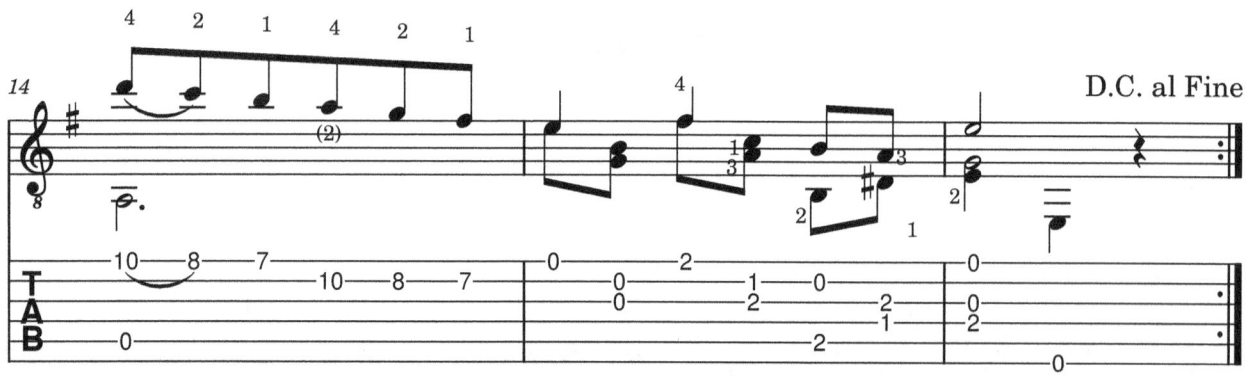

Etude No.1

Francisco Tarrega (1852-1909)

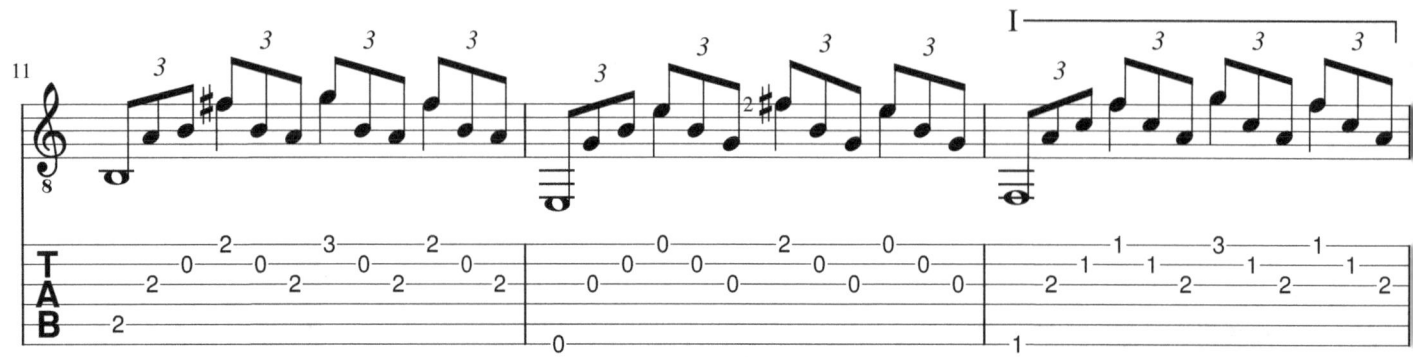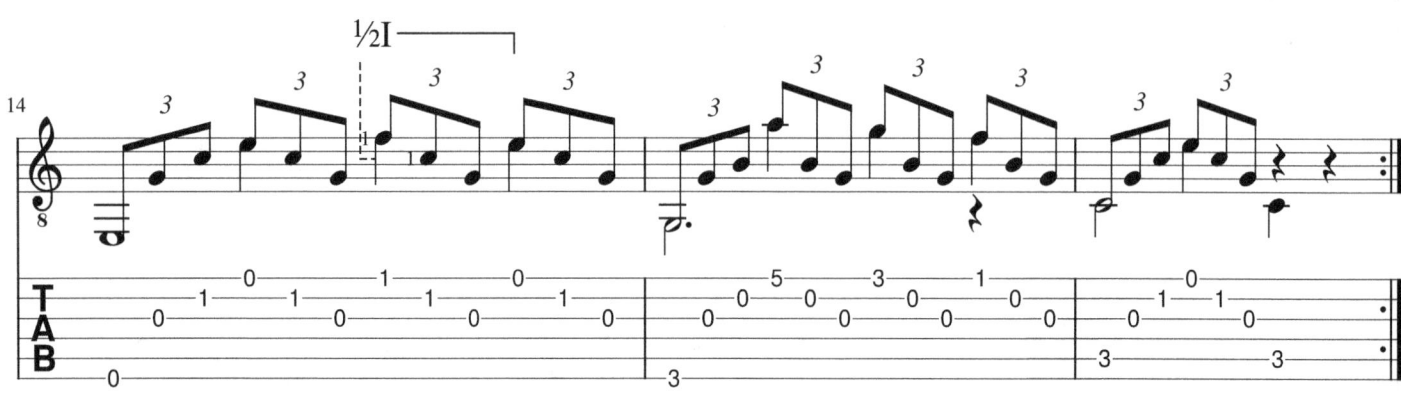

Adelita
Mazurka

Francisco Tarrega (1852-1909)

Estudio

Francisco Tarrega

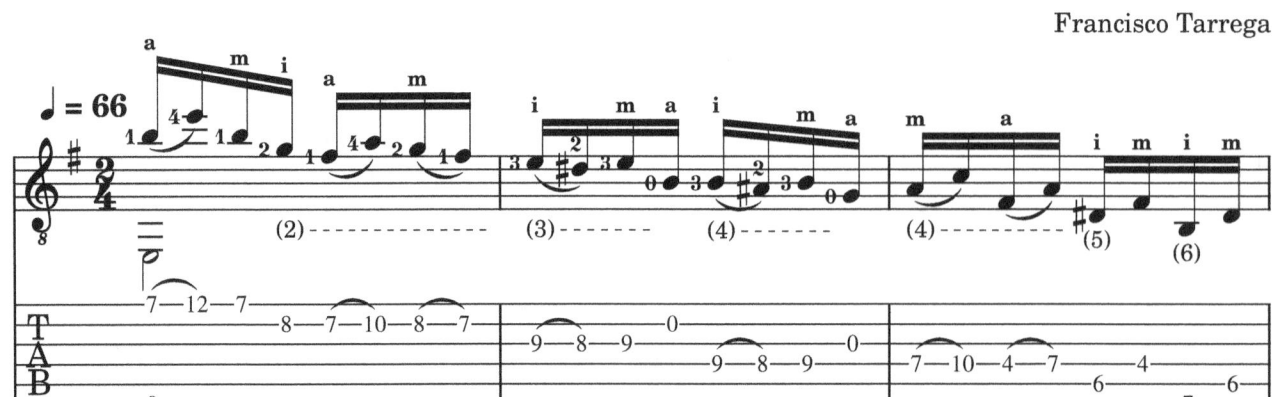
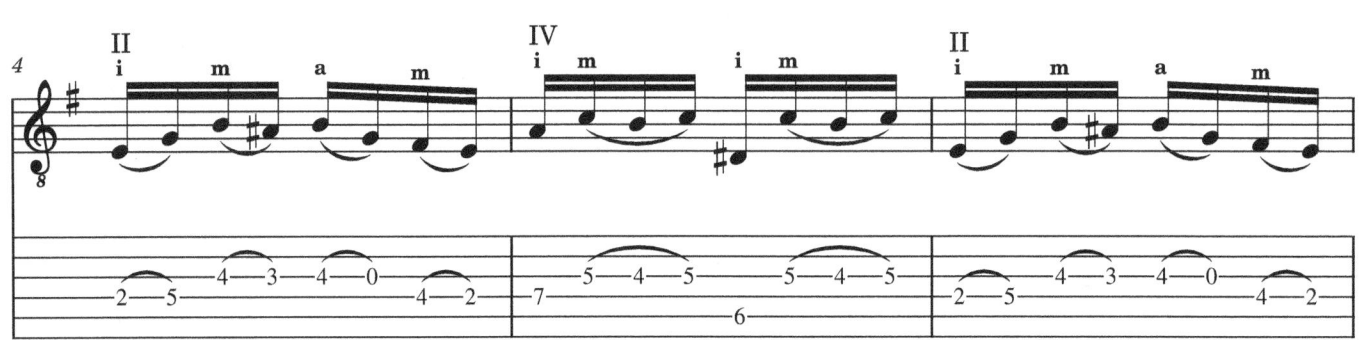
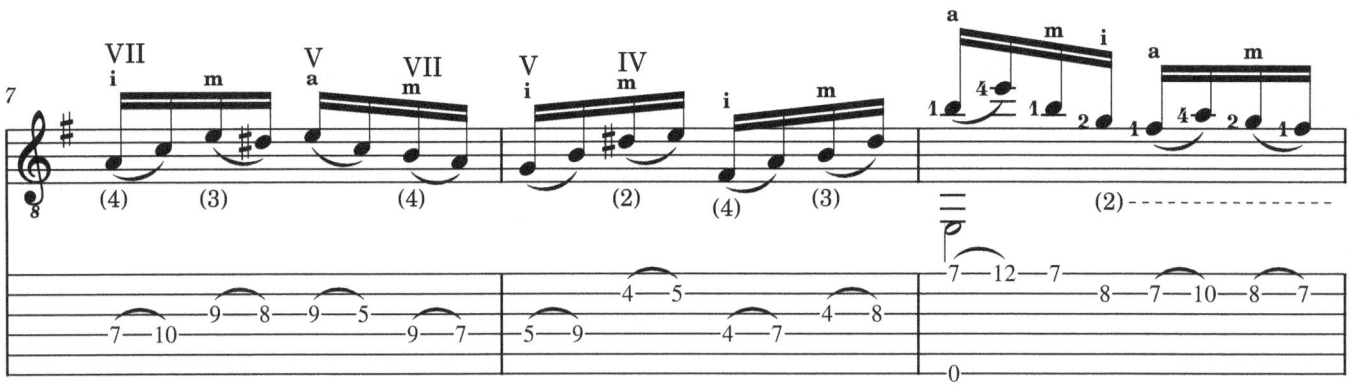
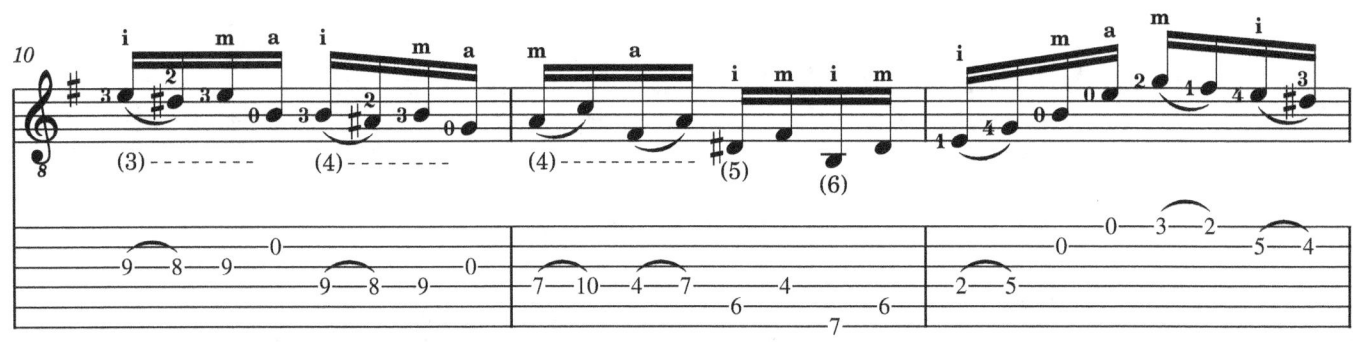

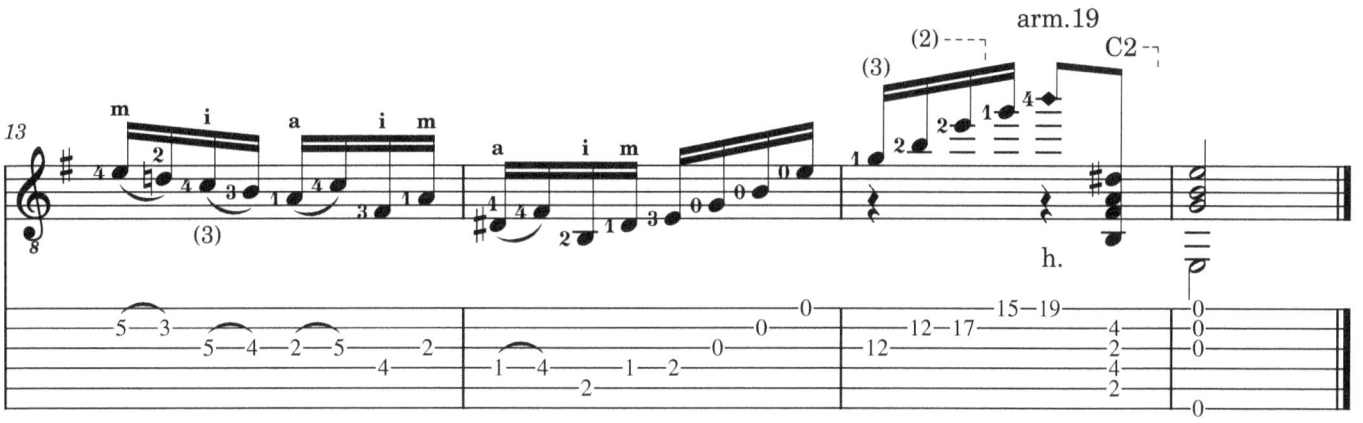

Etude

Francisco Tárrega (1852 - 1909)

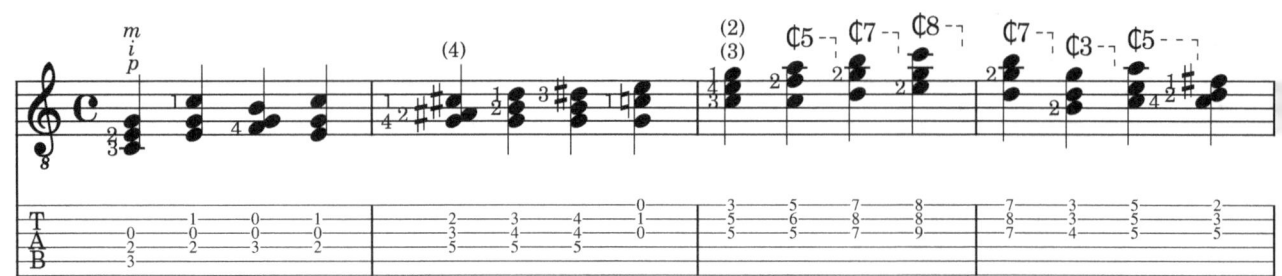
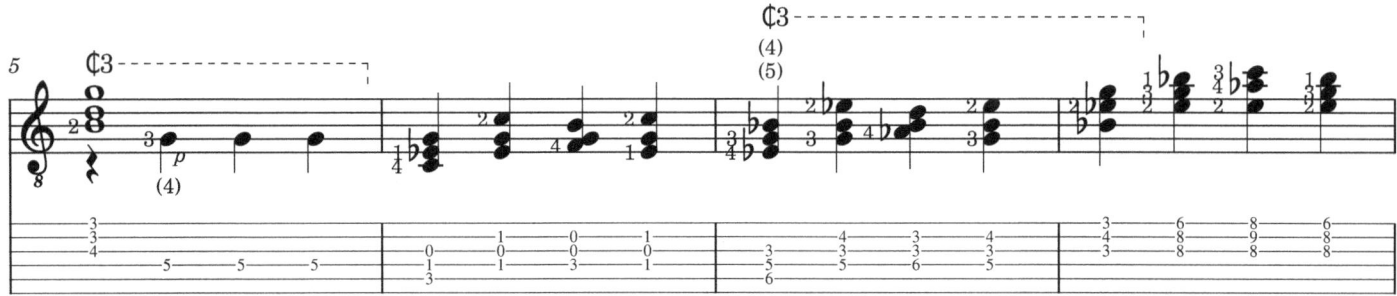
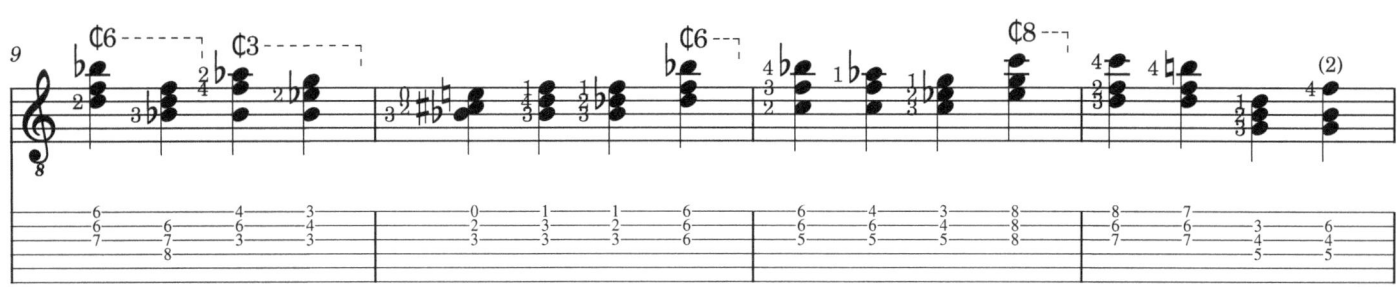
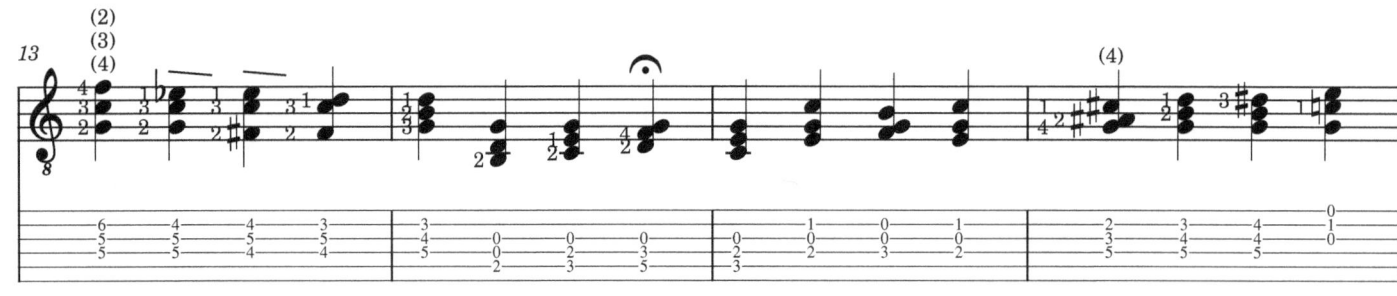
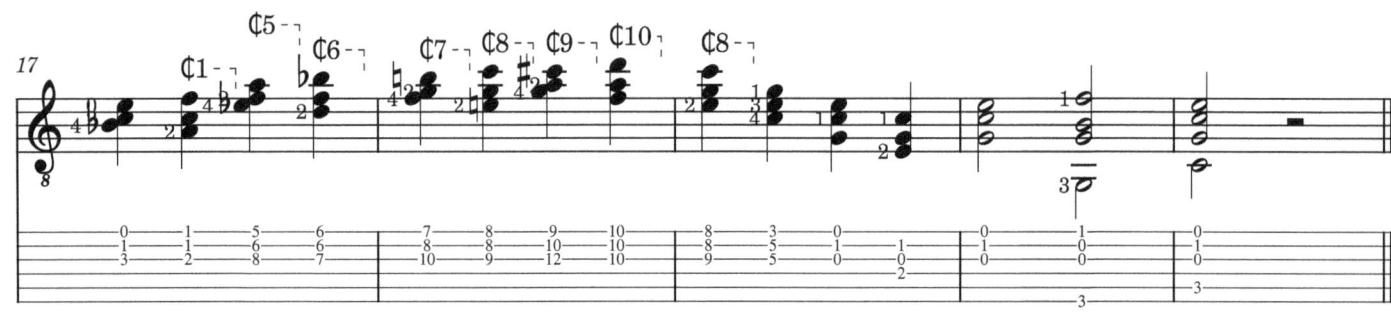

Etude in G

Johann Kaspar Mertz (1806 - 1856)

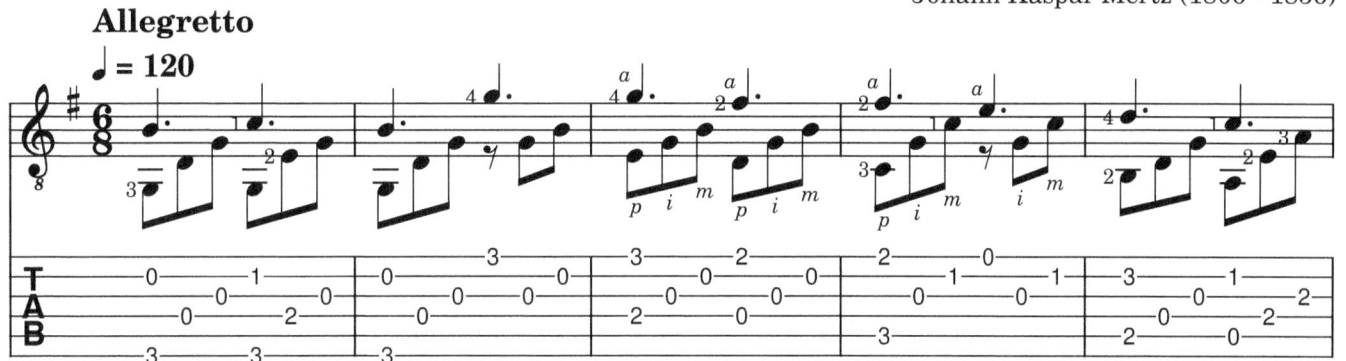
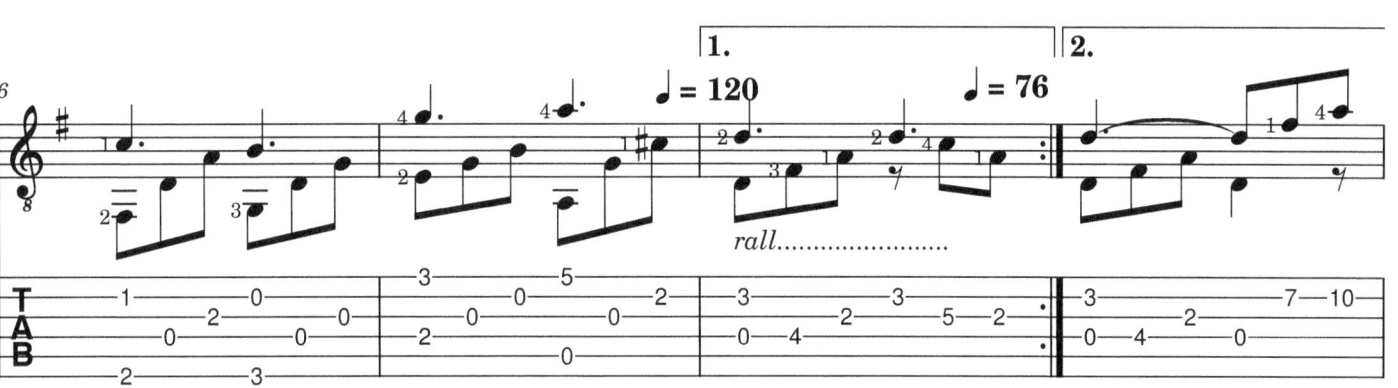
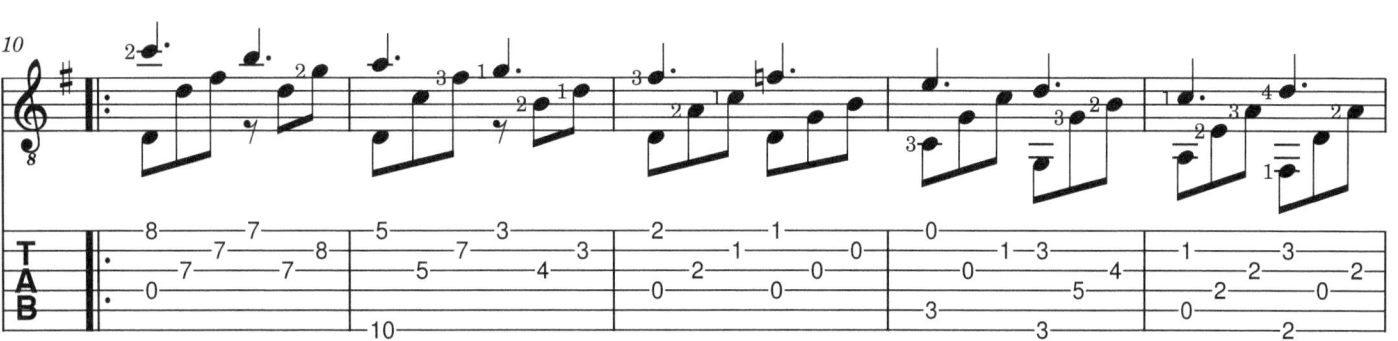
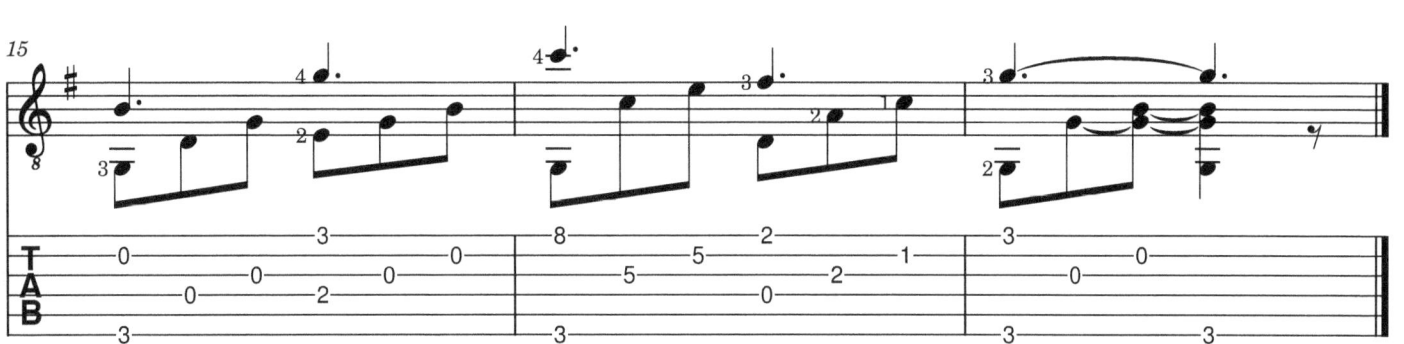

Ländler

Johann Kaspar Mertz (1806 - 1856)

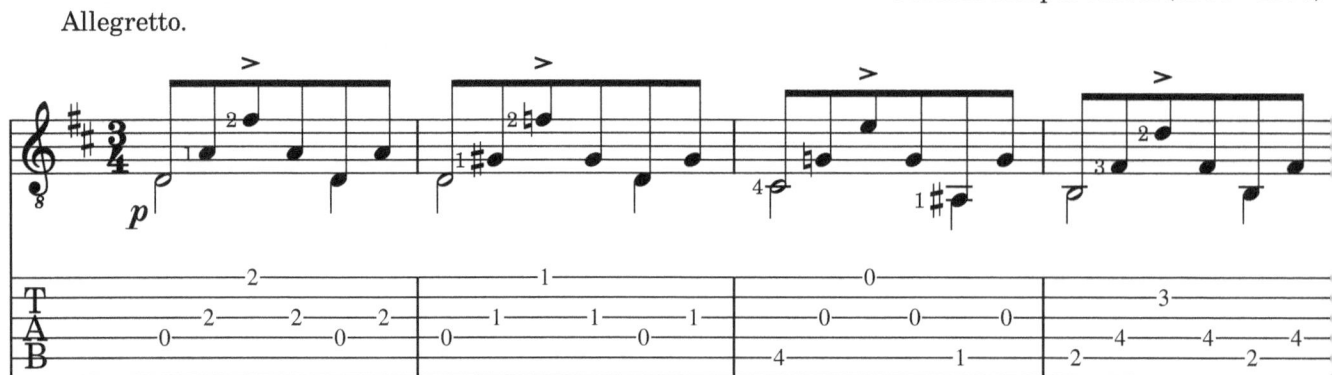
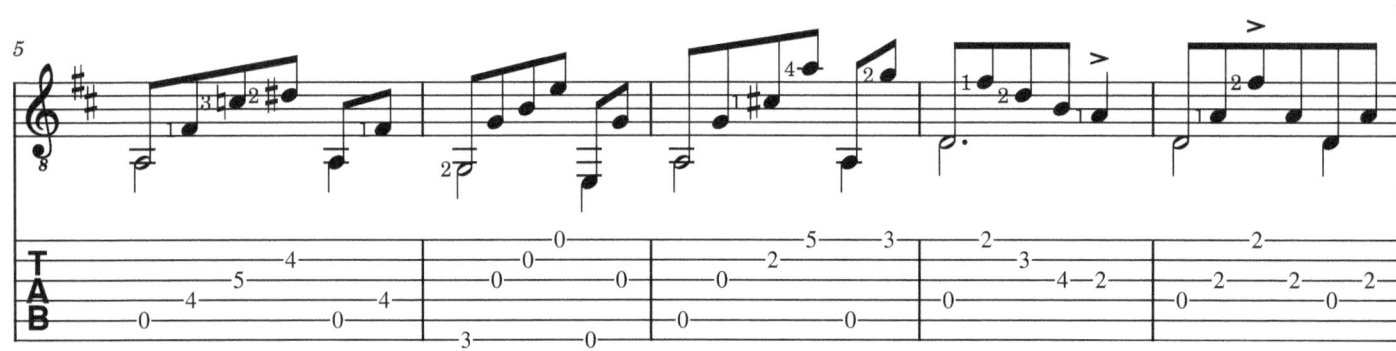
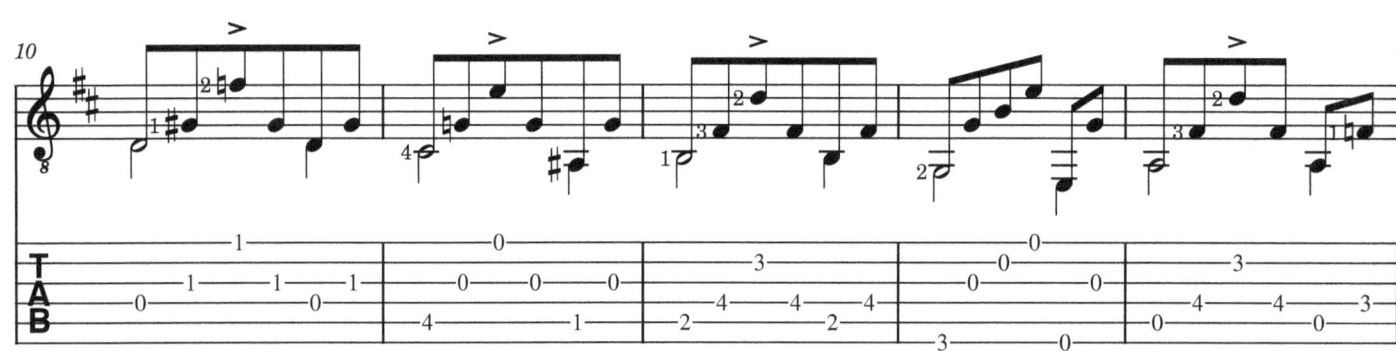
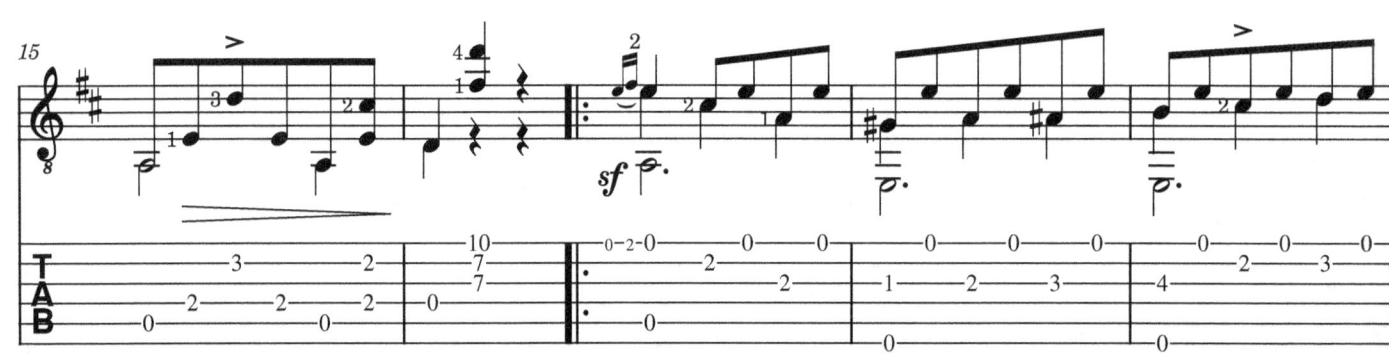

Romance

Johann Kaspar Mertz (1806 - 1856)

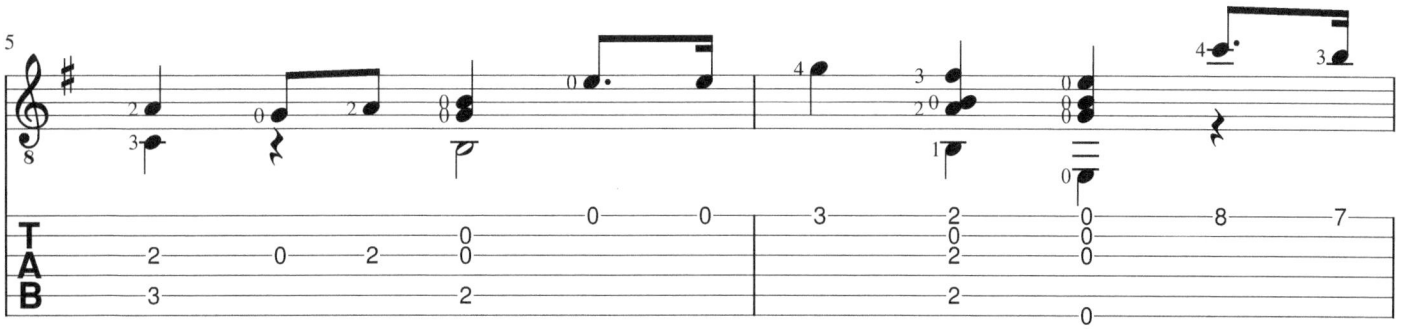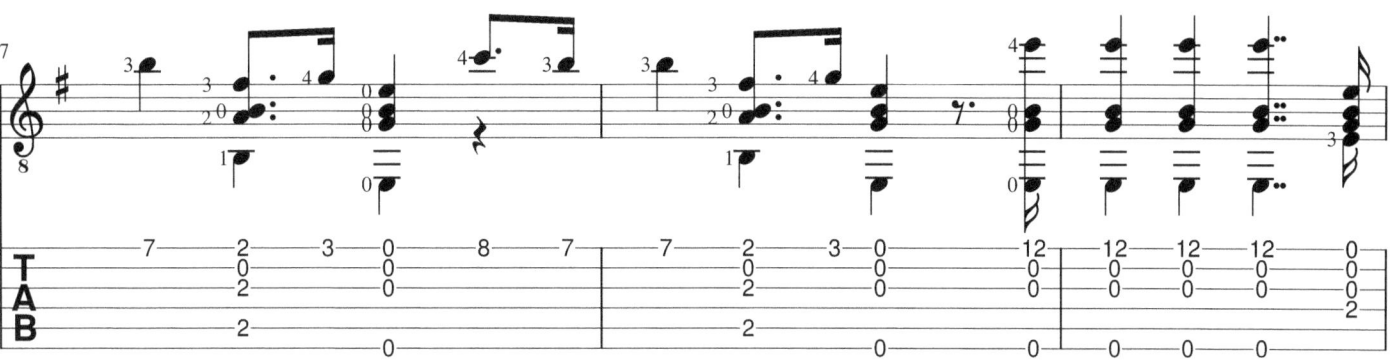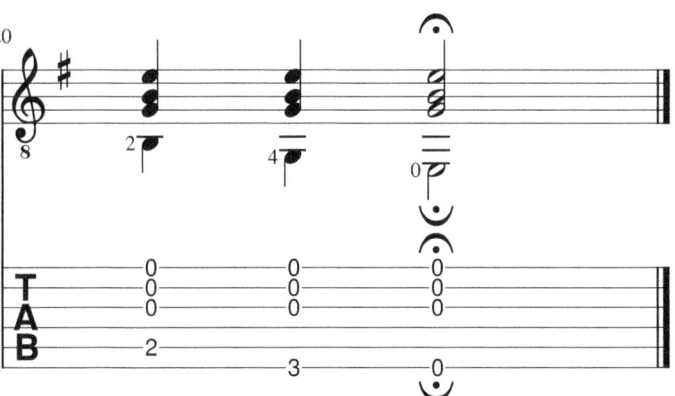

Nocturne
Opus 4 No.2 Part1

Johann Kaspar Mertz (1806 - 1856)

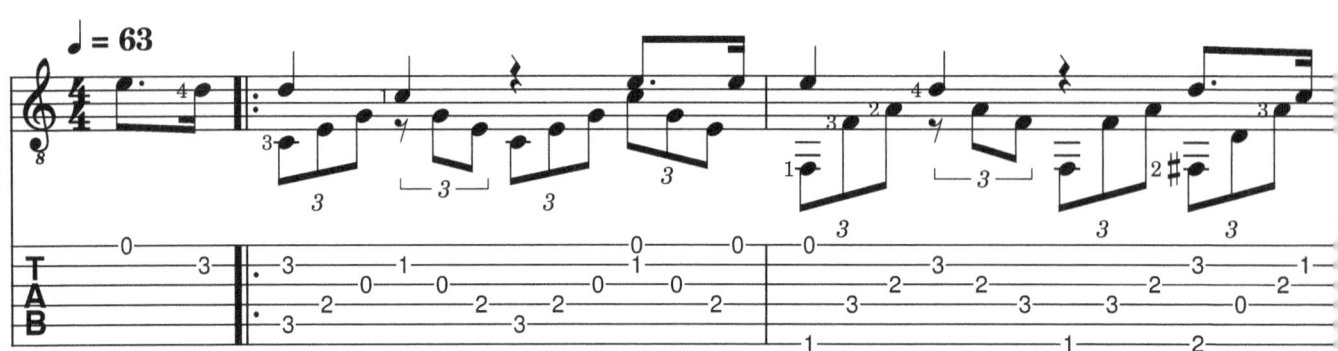

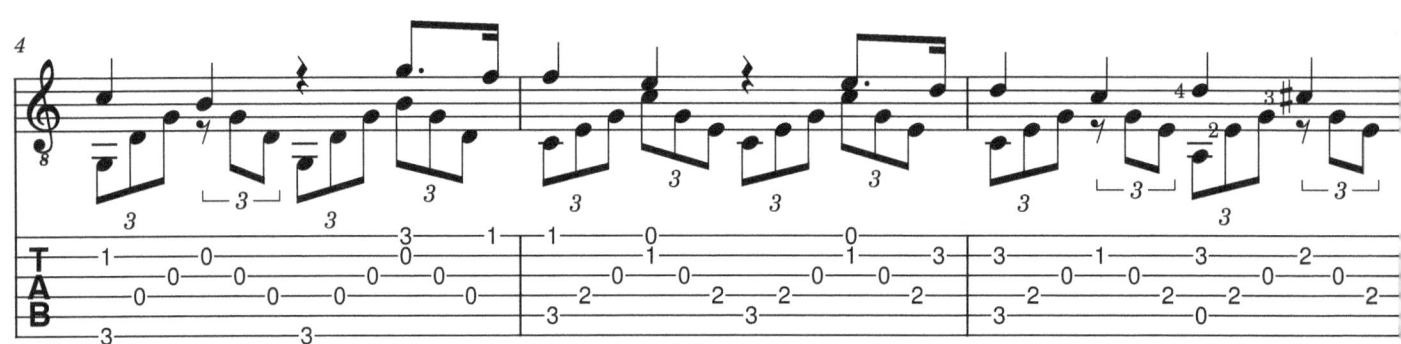

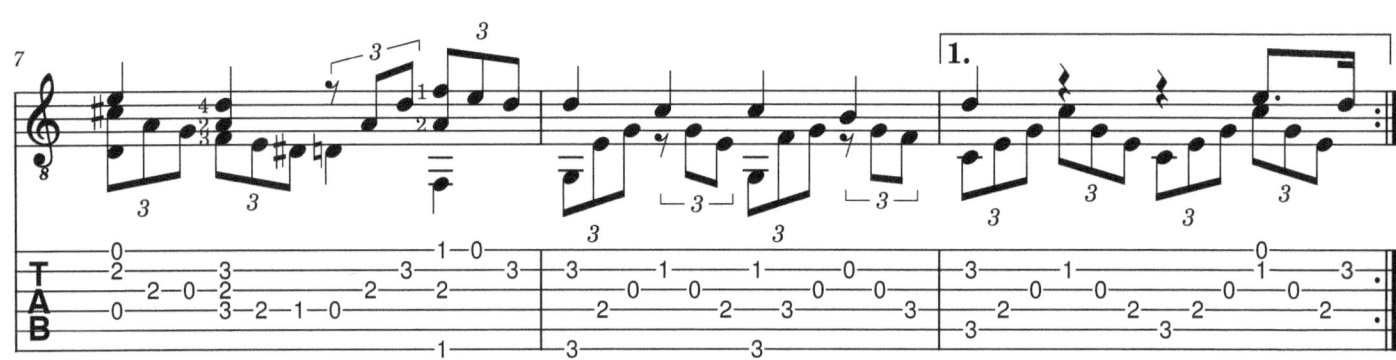

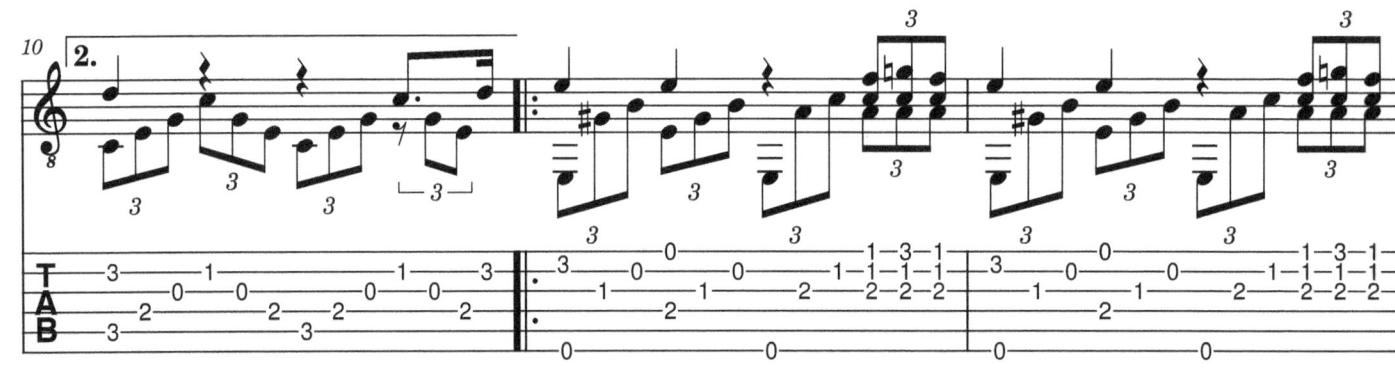

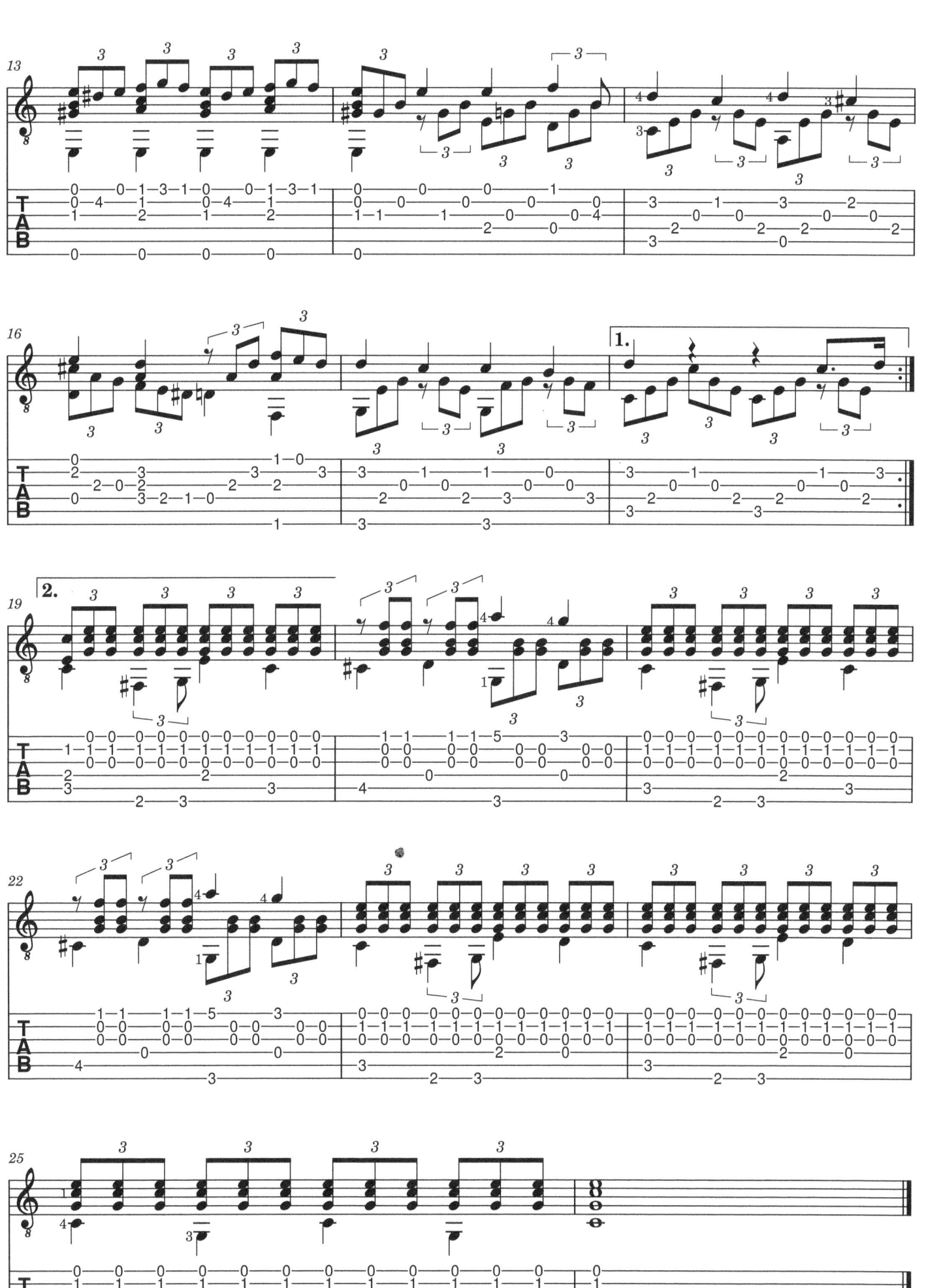

Polonaise No.6, Op.13

Johann Kaspar Mertz (1806 - 1856)

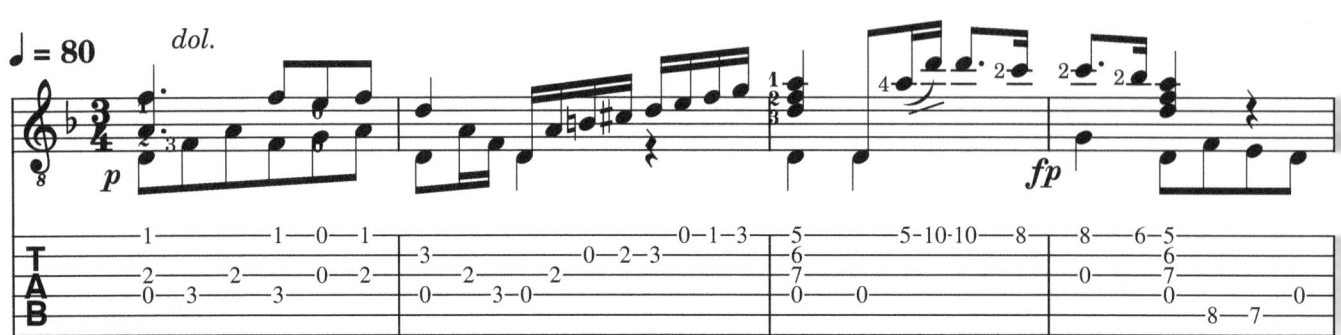
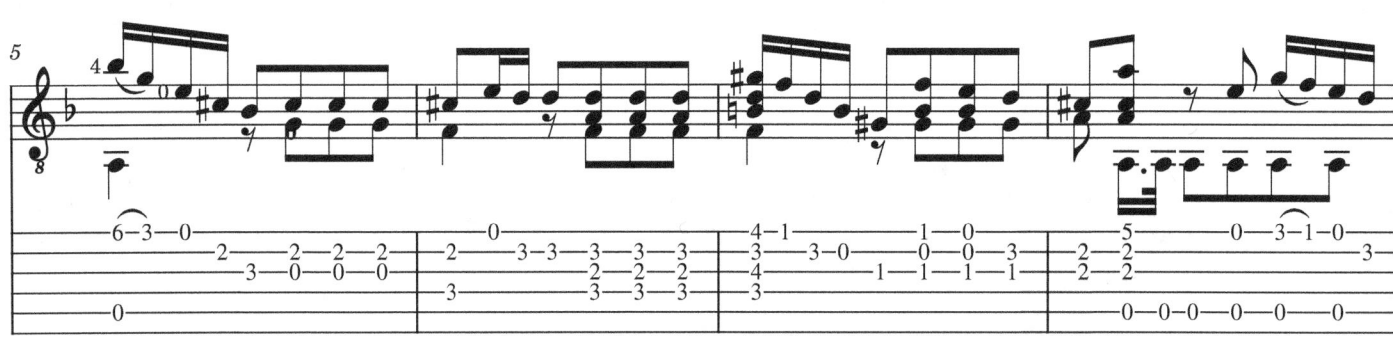
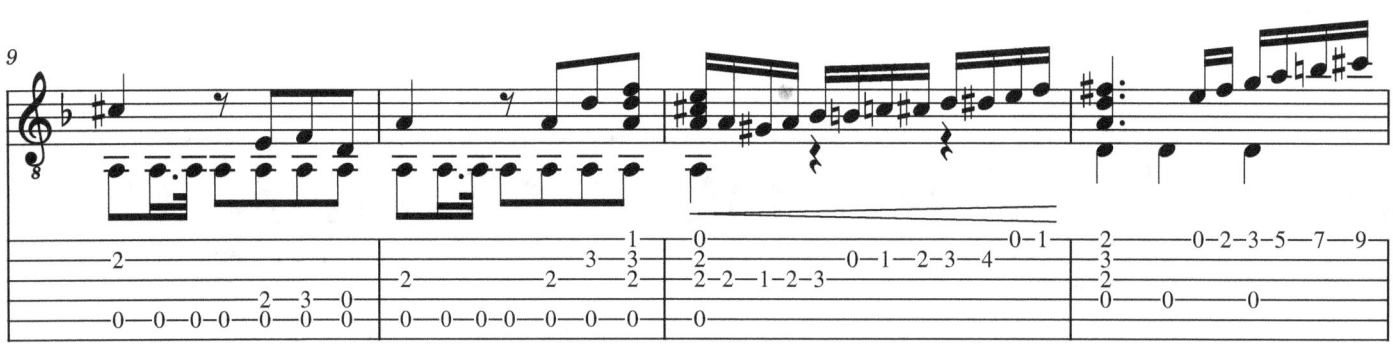
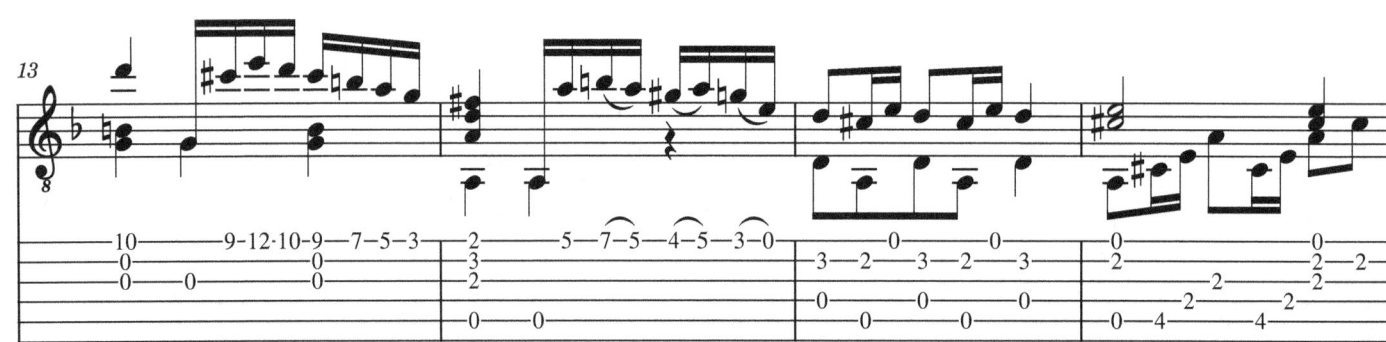

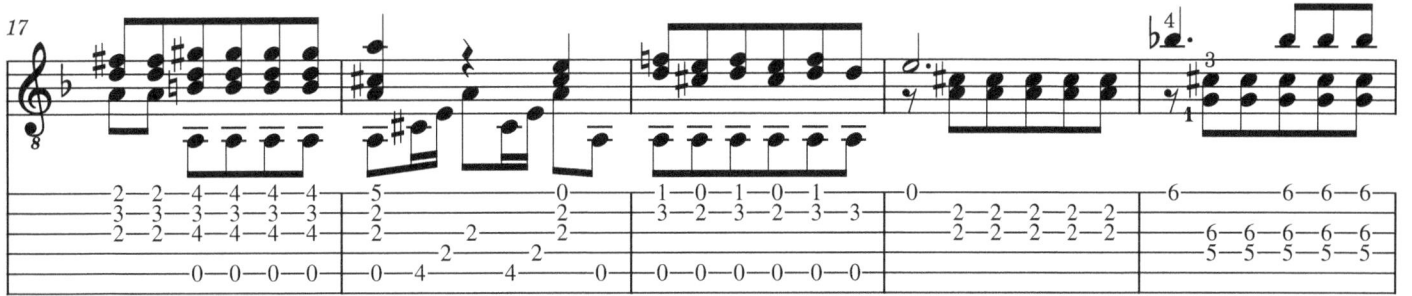
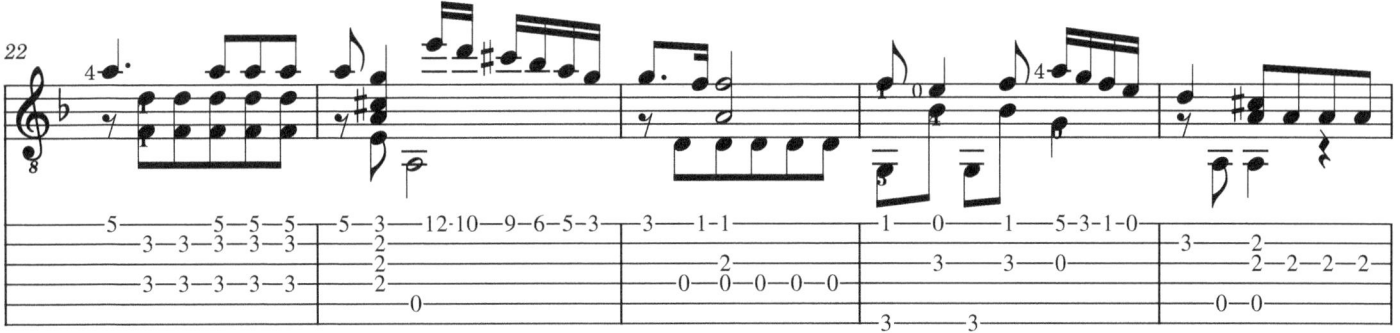
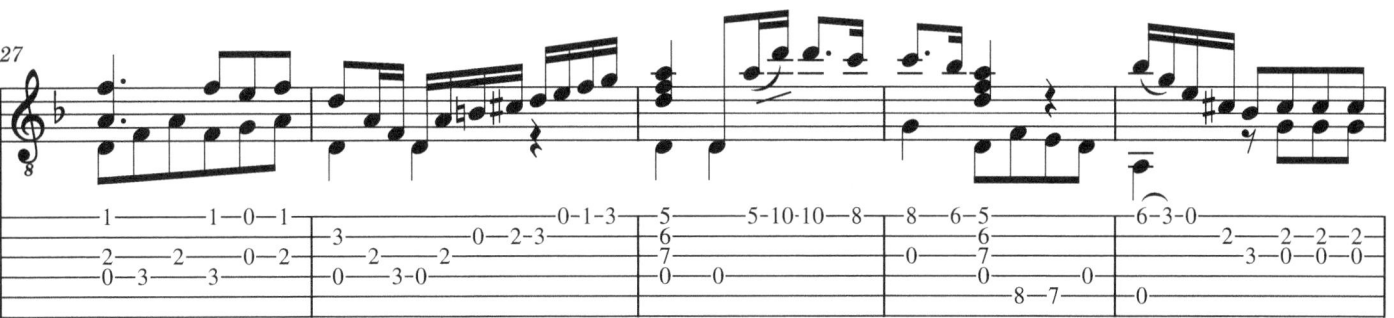
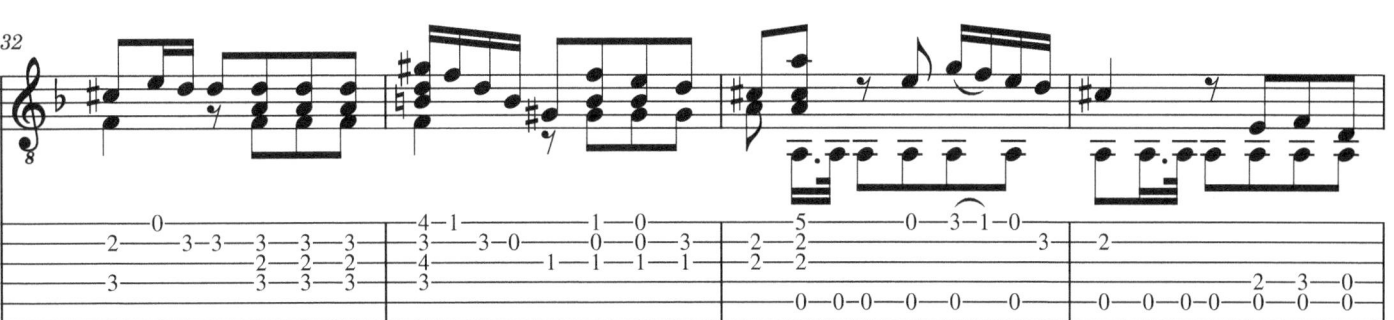
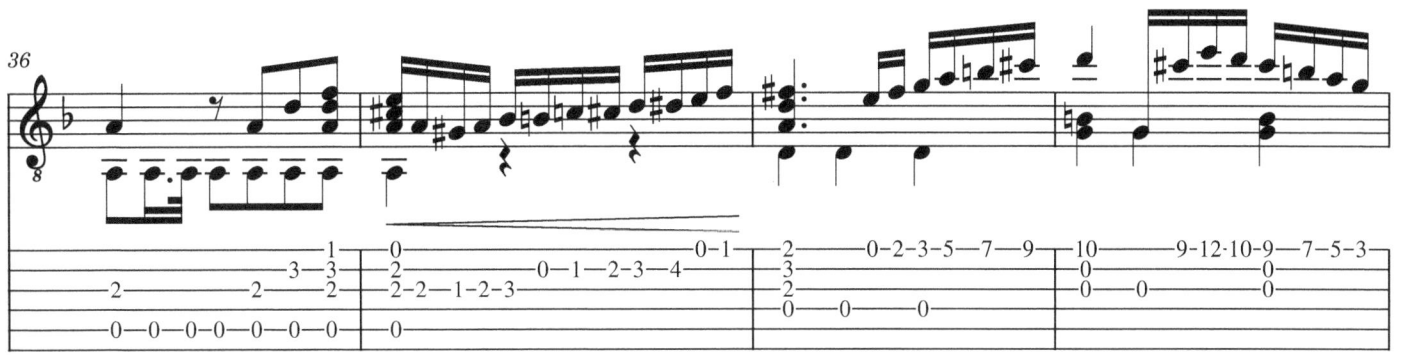

Trio

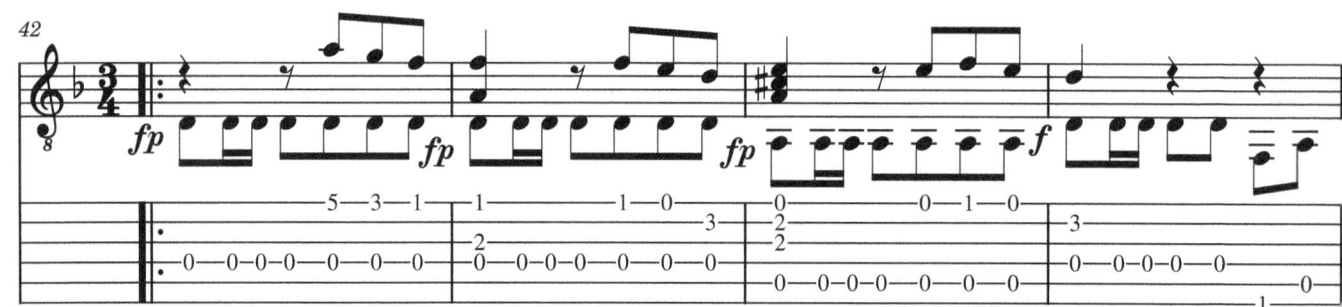

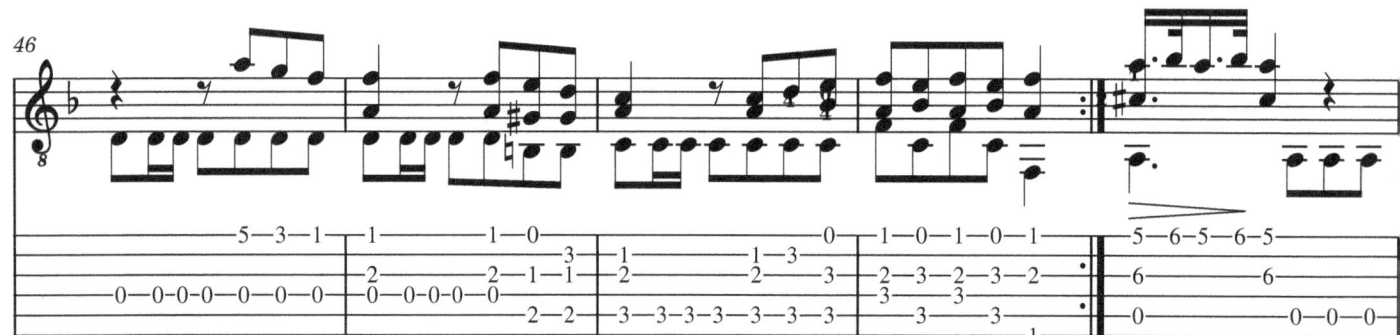

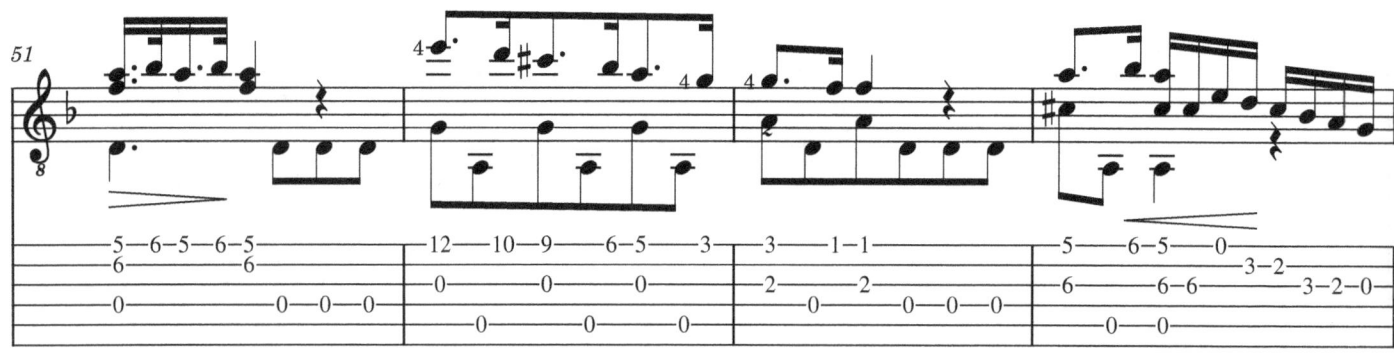

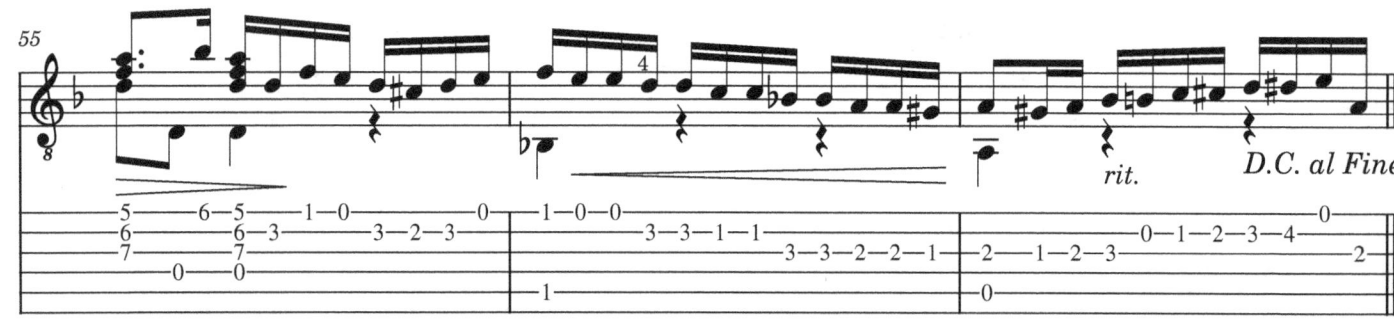

Ejercicio

Jose Ferrer (1835 - 1916)

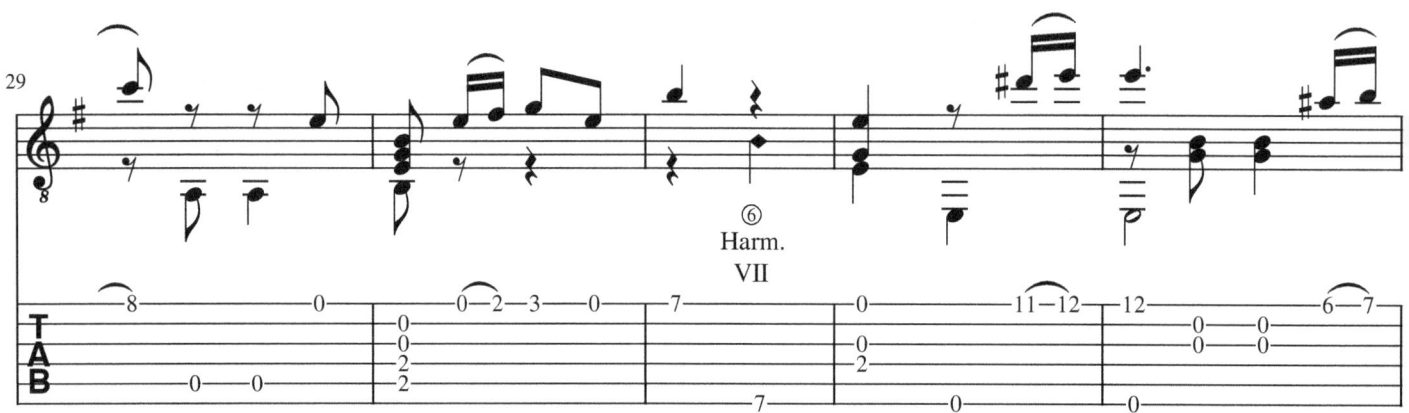
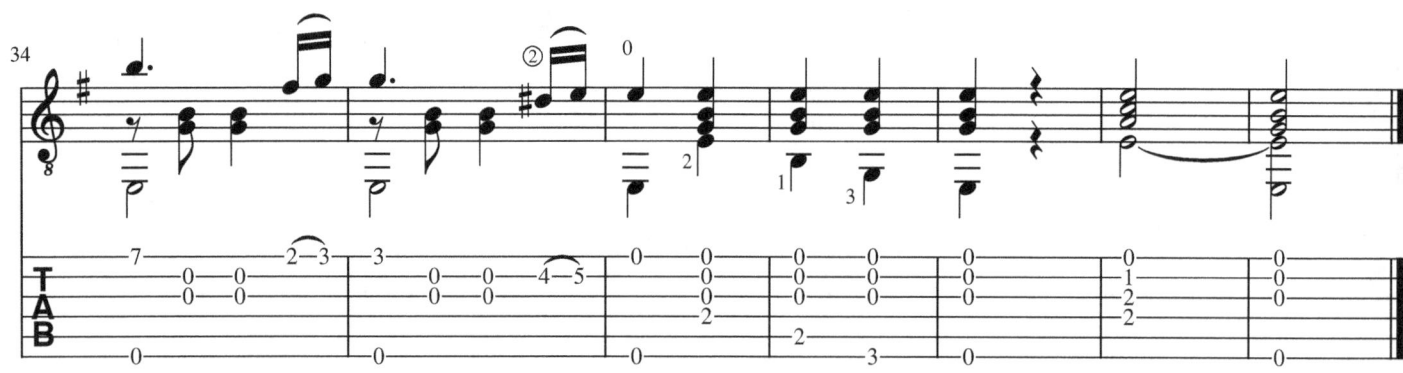

EL Amable

José Ferrer (1835 - 1916)

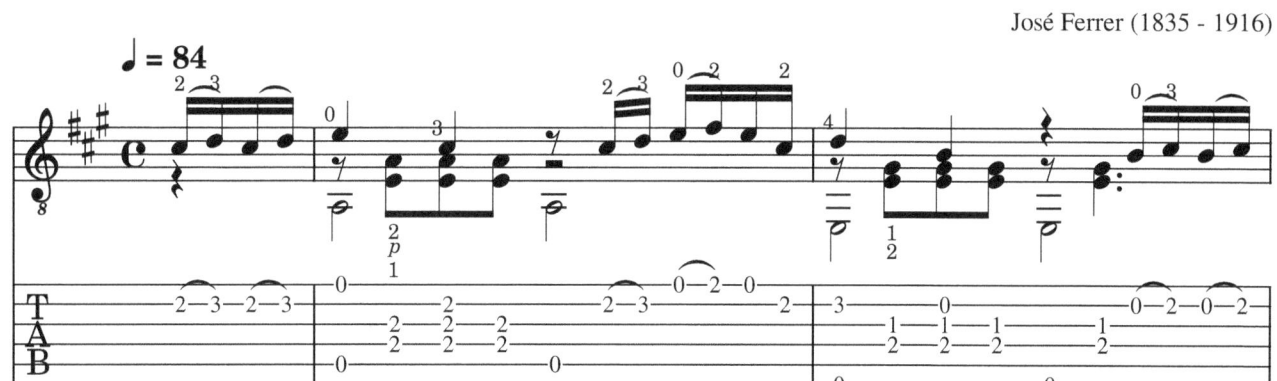

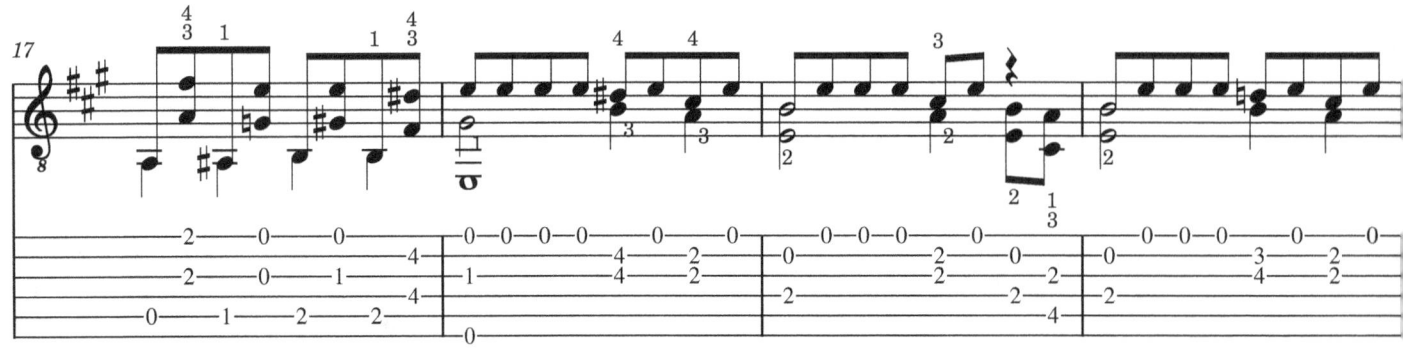

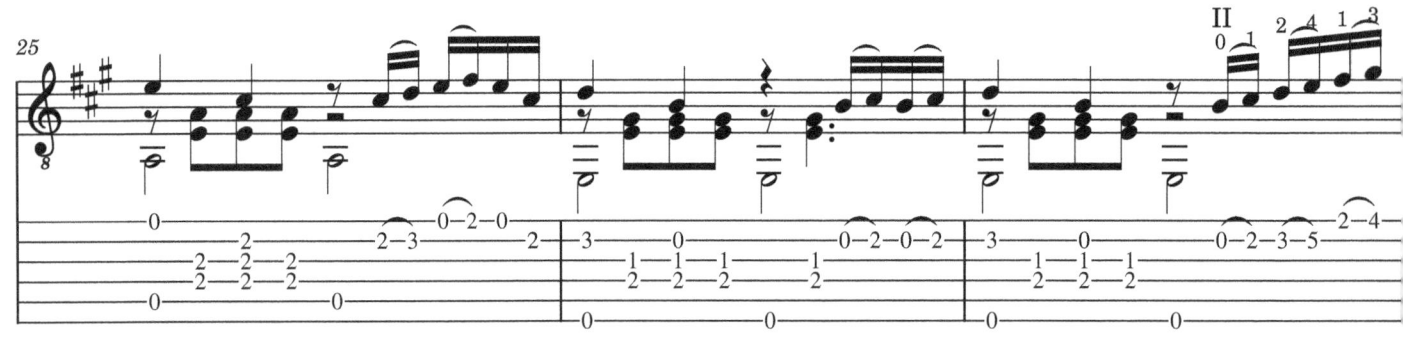
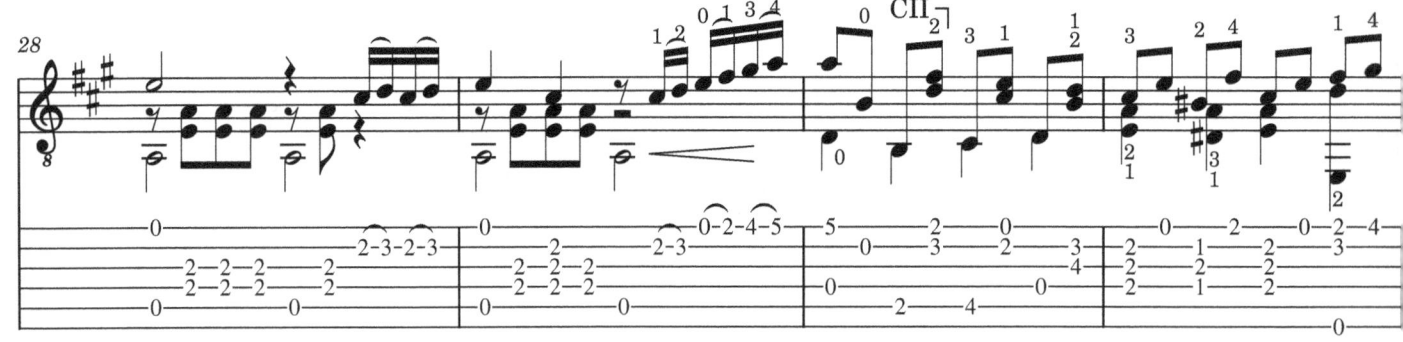
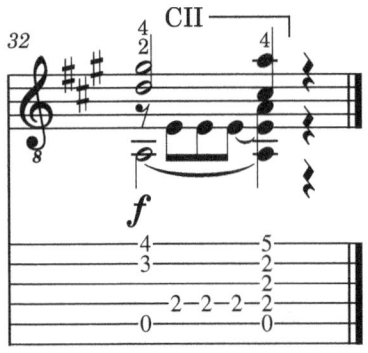

Tango n°3 op.50

Jose Ferrer (1835 - 1916)

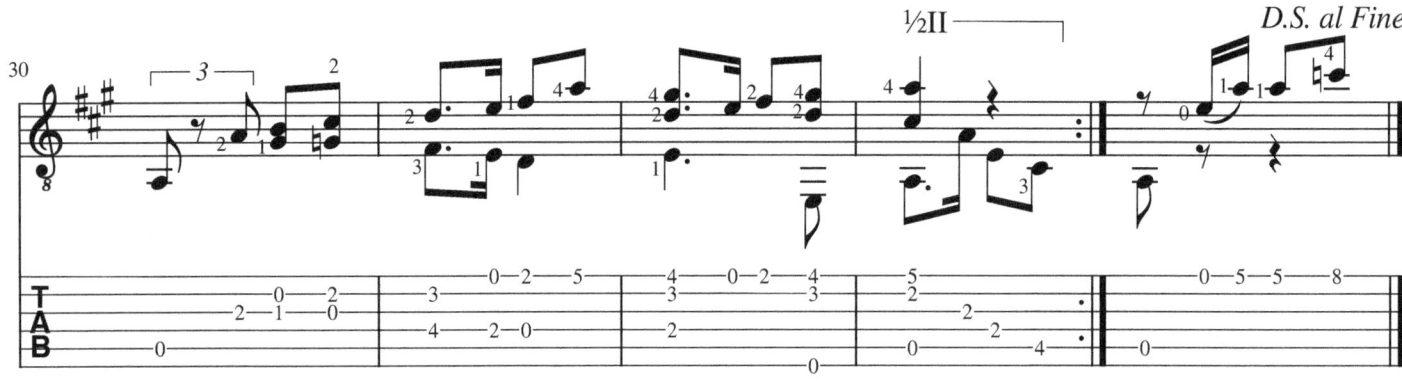

45

Tango No.1

Julian Arcas (1832 - 1882)

Aire de Tango

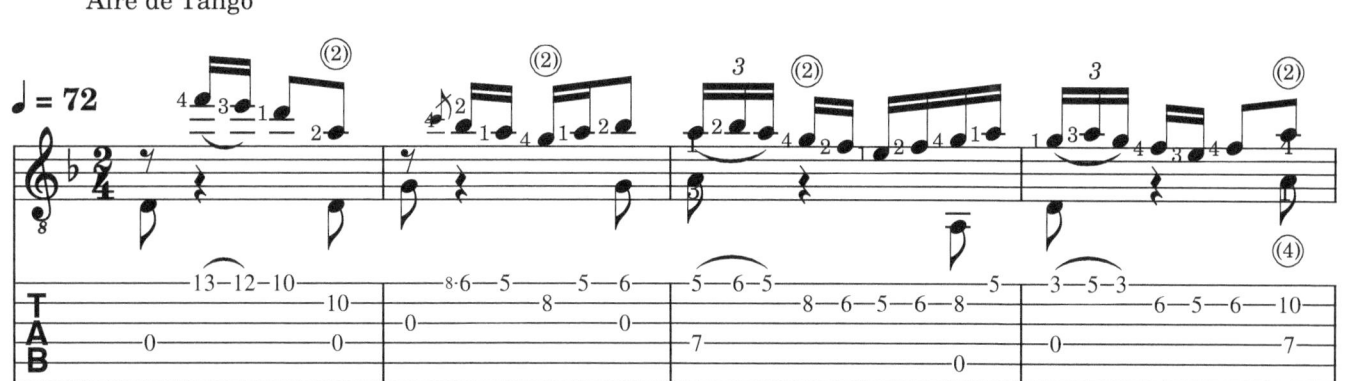
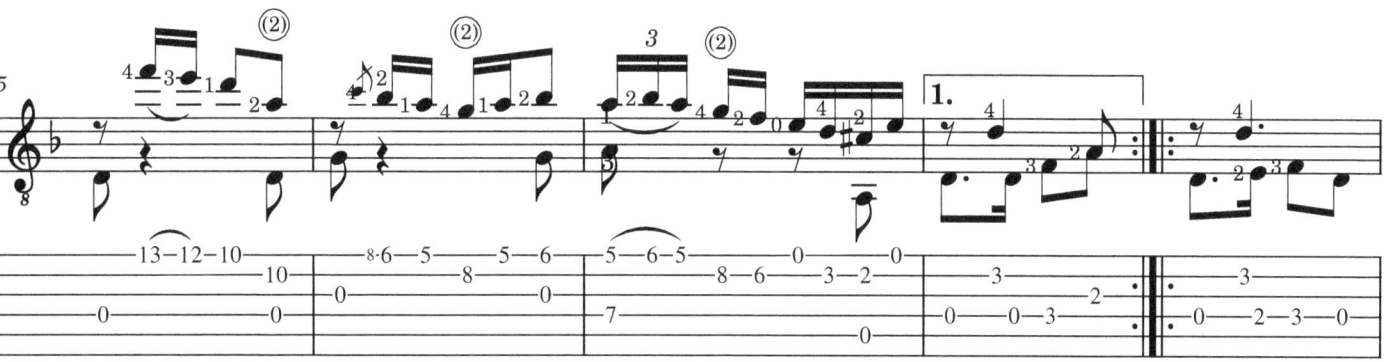
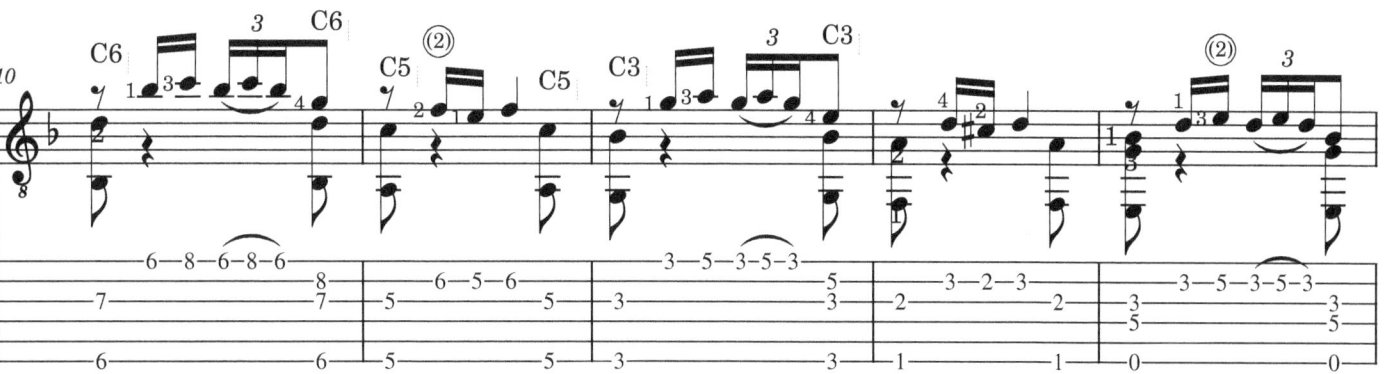
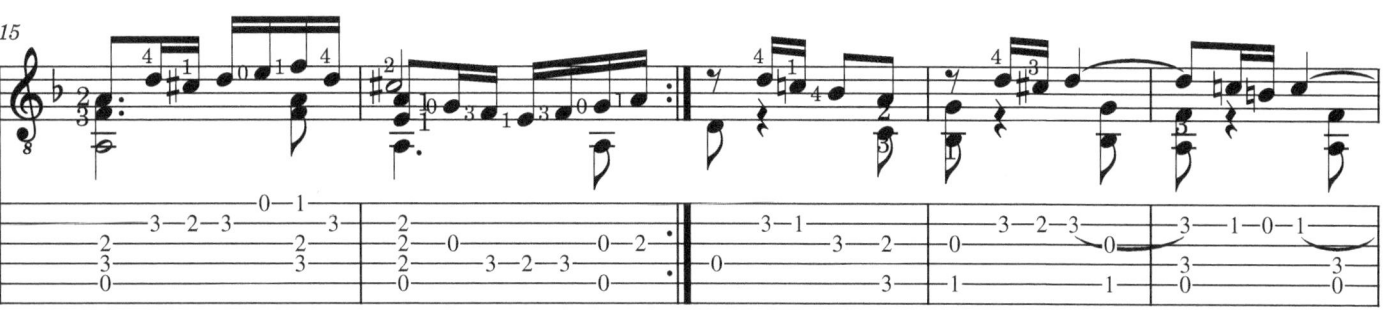

Bolero

Julian Arcas (1832 - 1882)

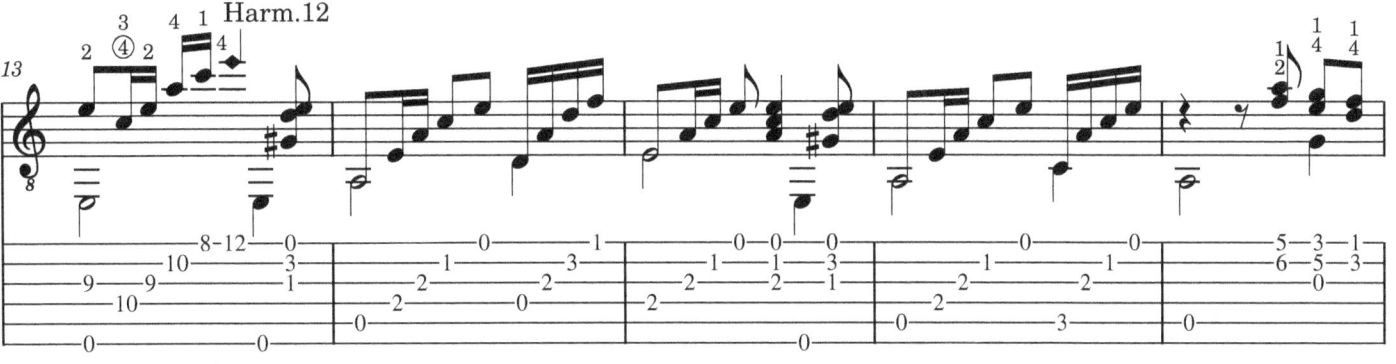
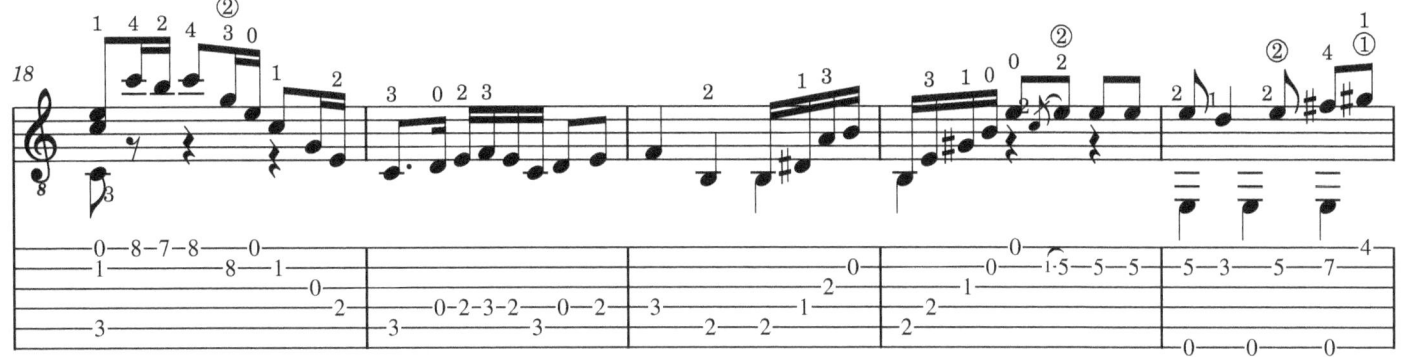

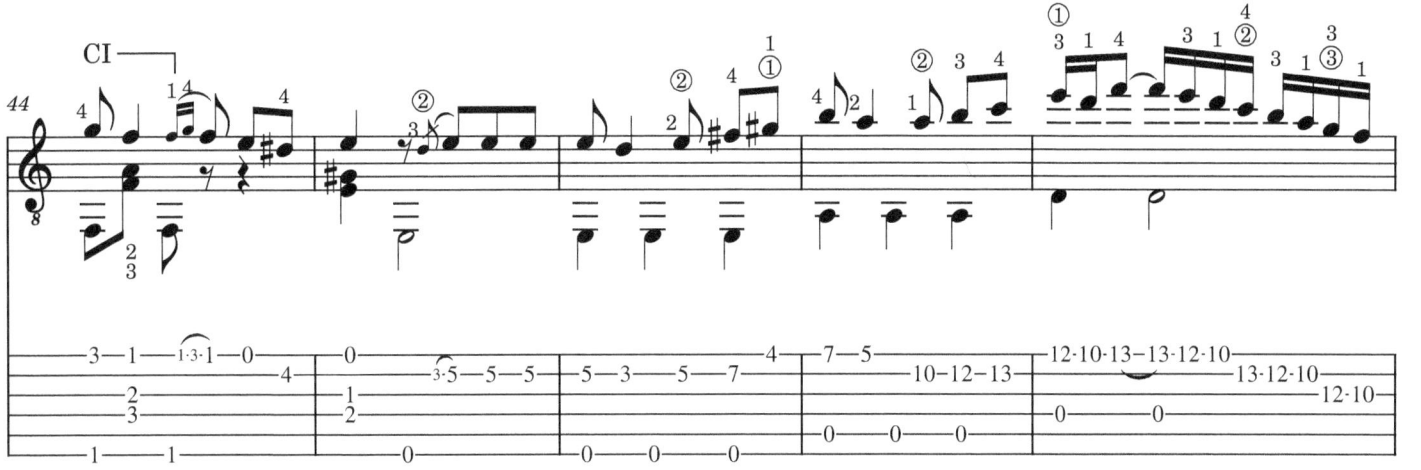
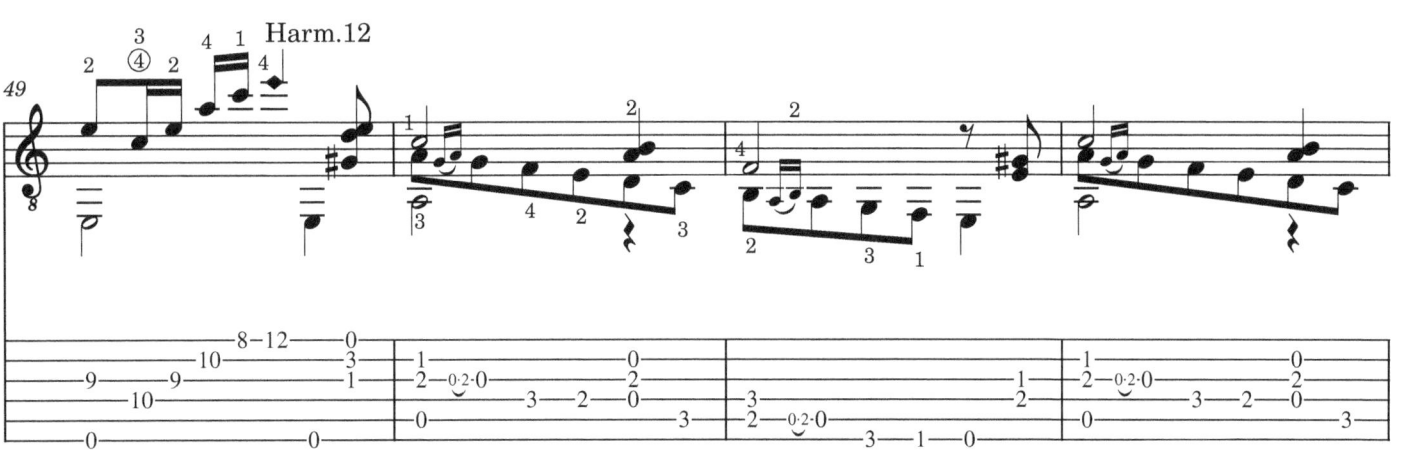
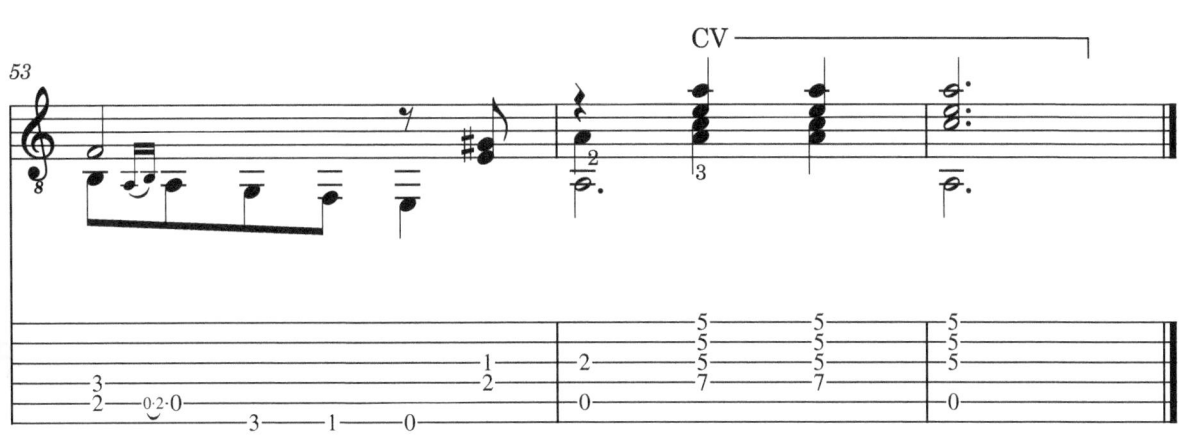

Tango No.4
Coleccion de 5 tangos

Julián Arcas (1832 - 1882)

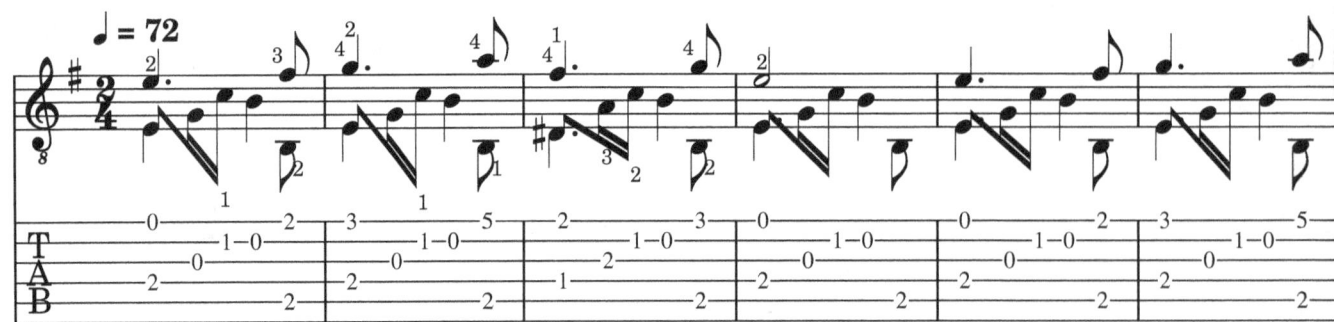
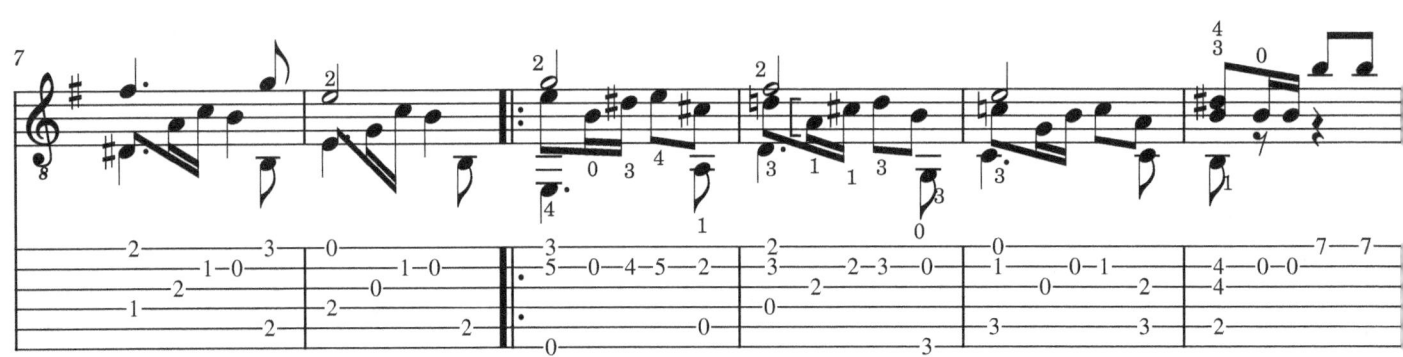

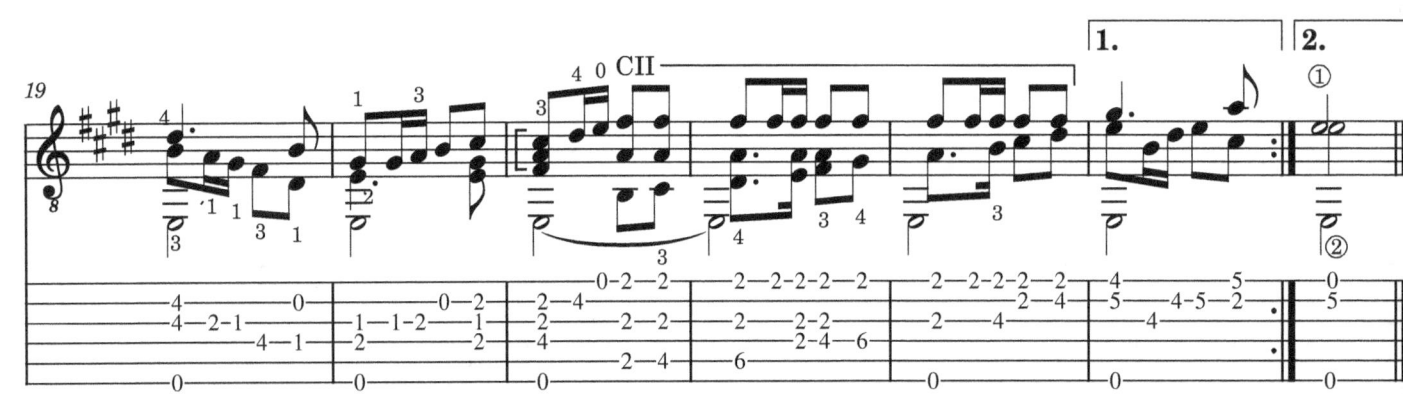

Habanera
A modern method for the guitar Vol.I

Pascual Roch (1864 - 1921)

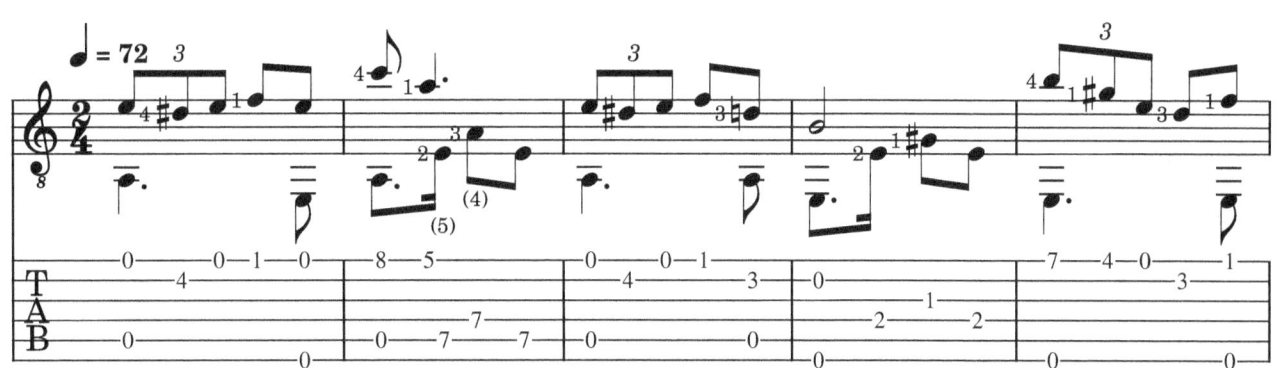
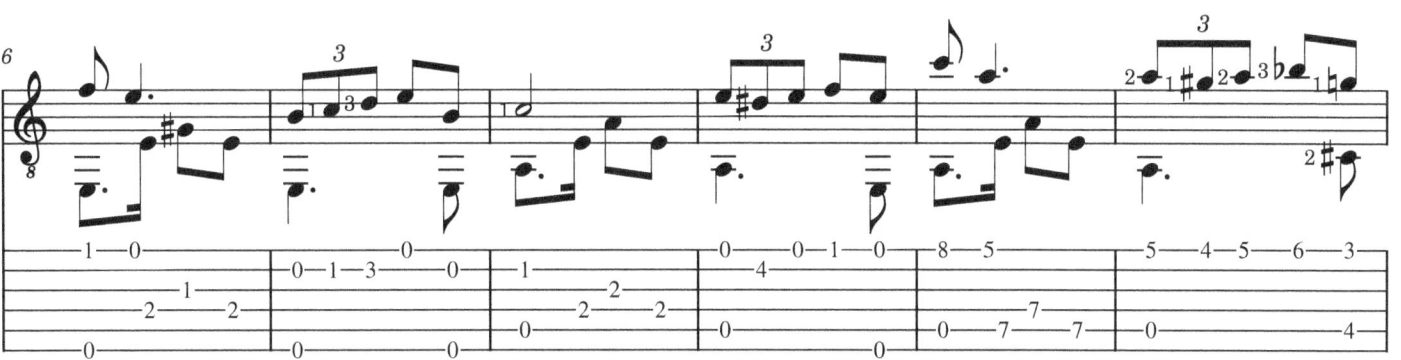

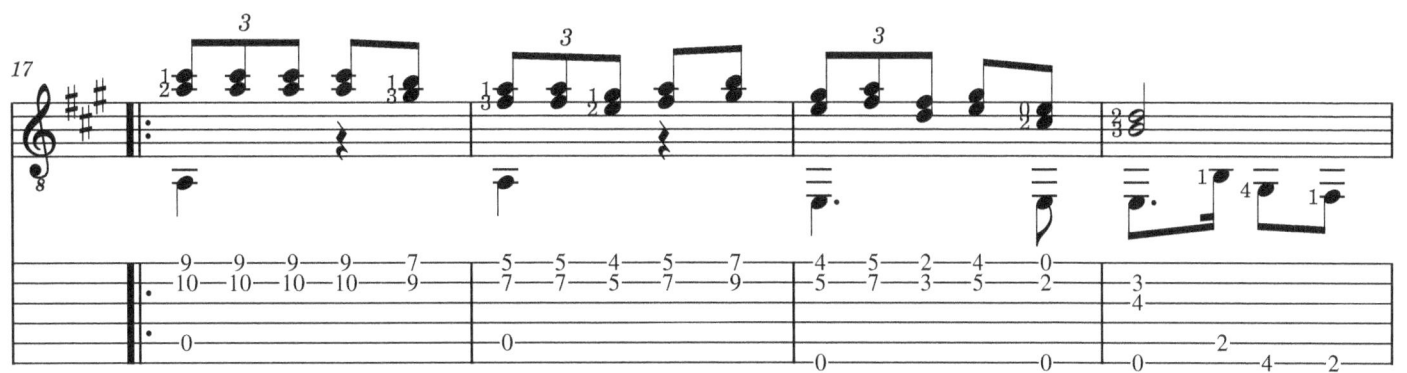

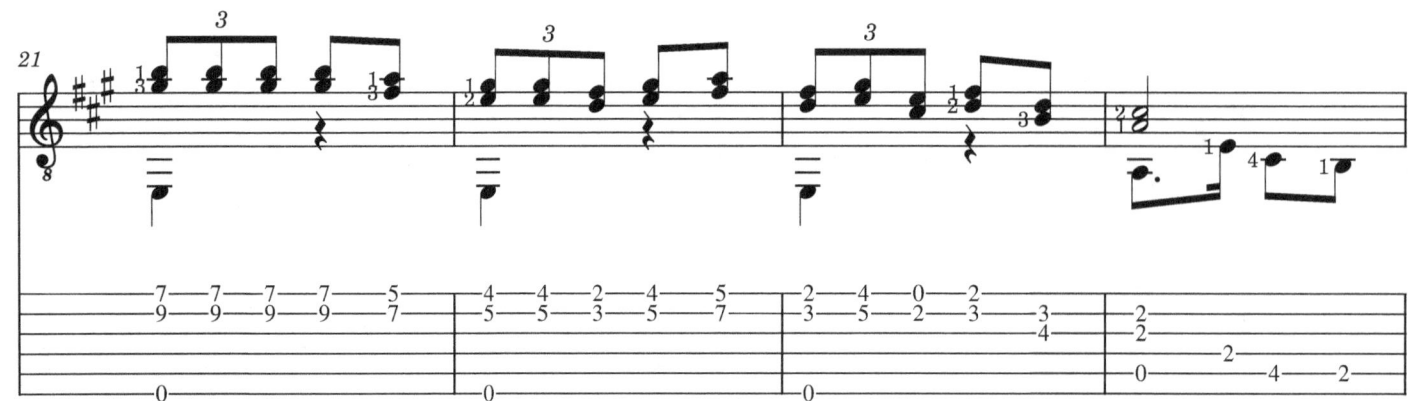
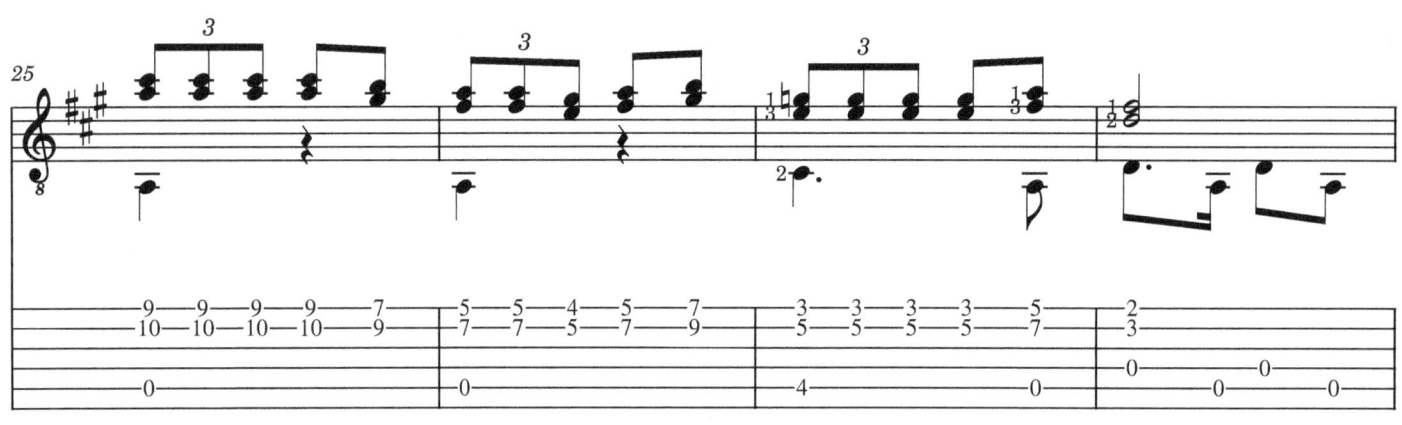
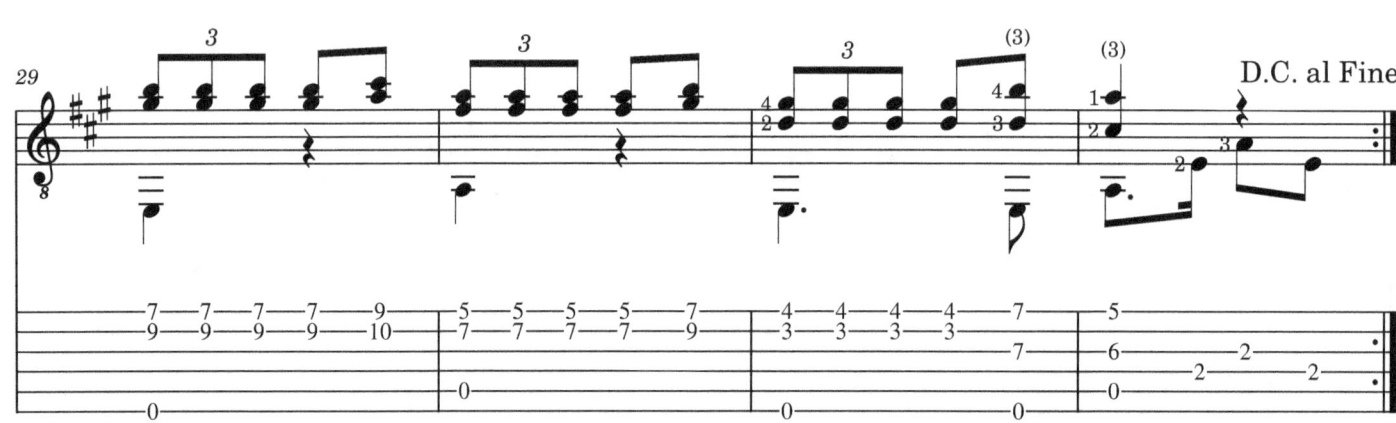

Valse

Pascual Roch (1864 - 1921)

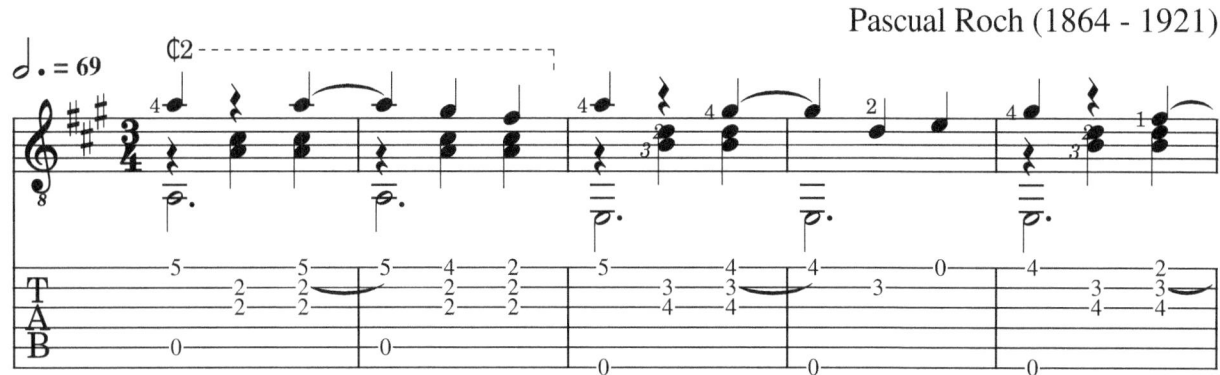
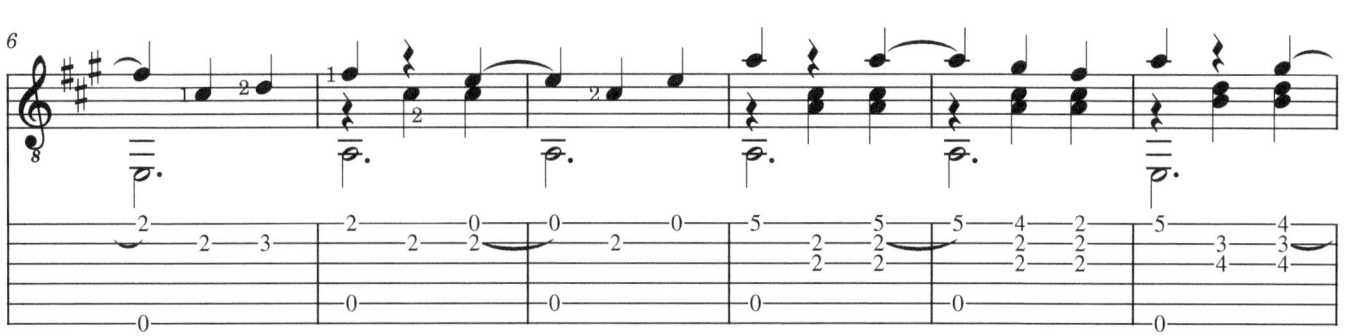
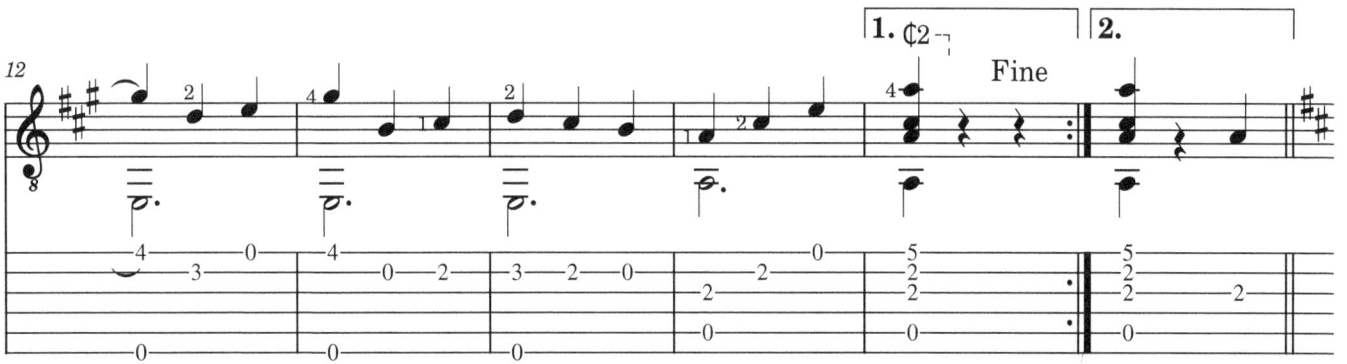
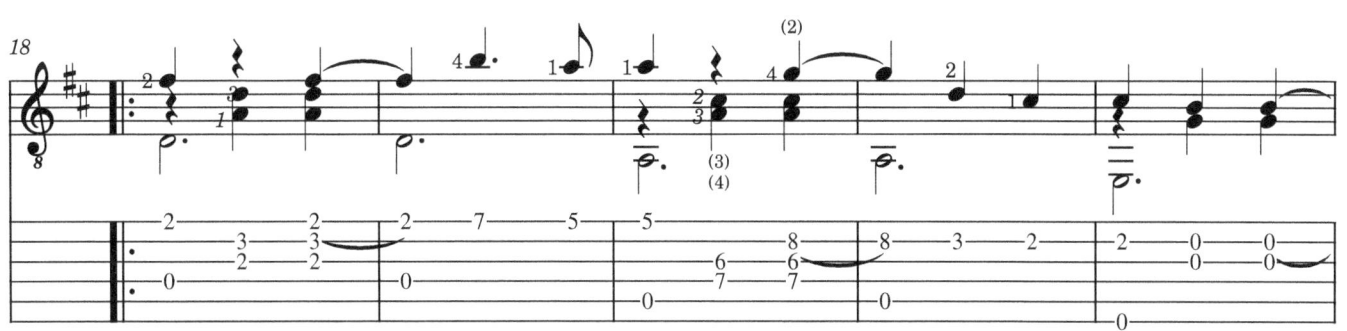

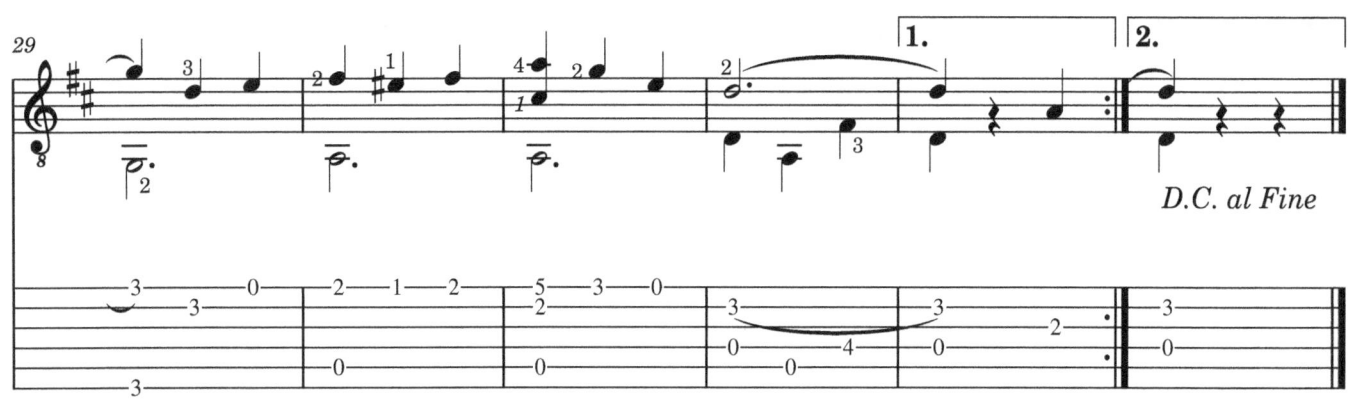

Etude n°14 op.35

Fernando Sor (1778 - 1839)

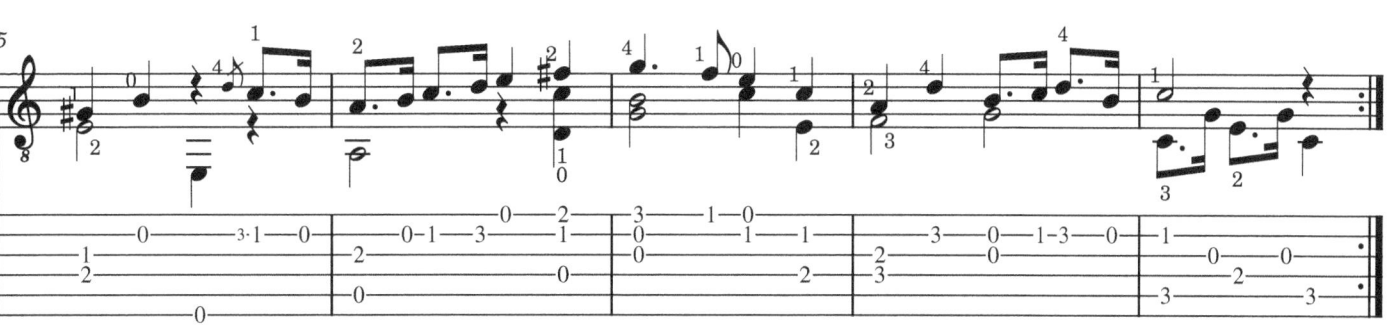

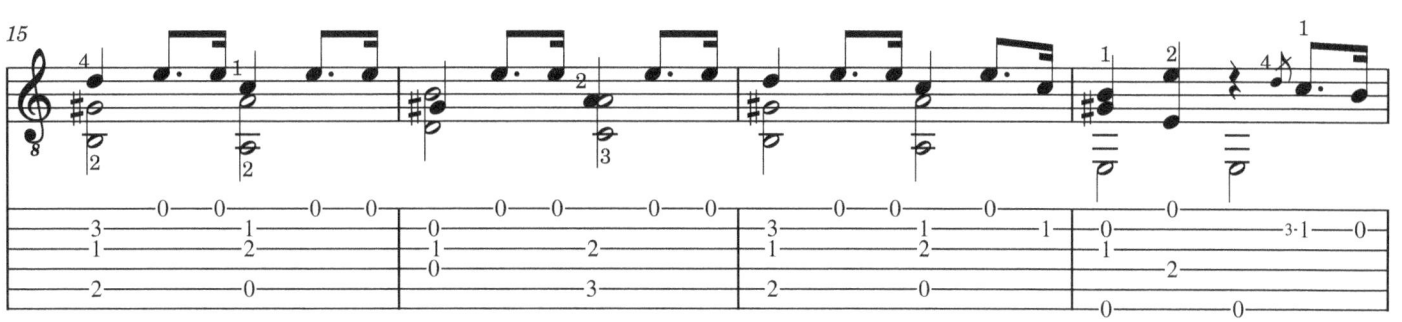

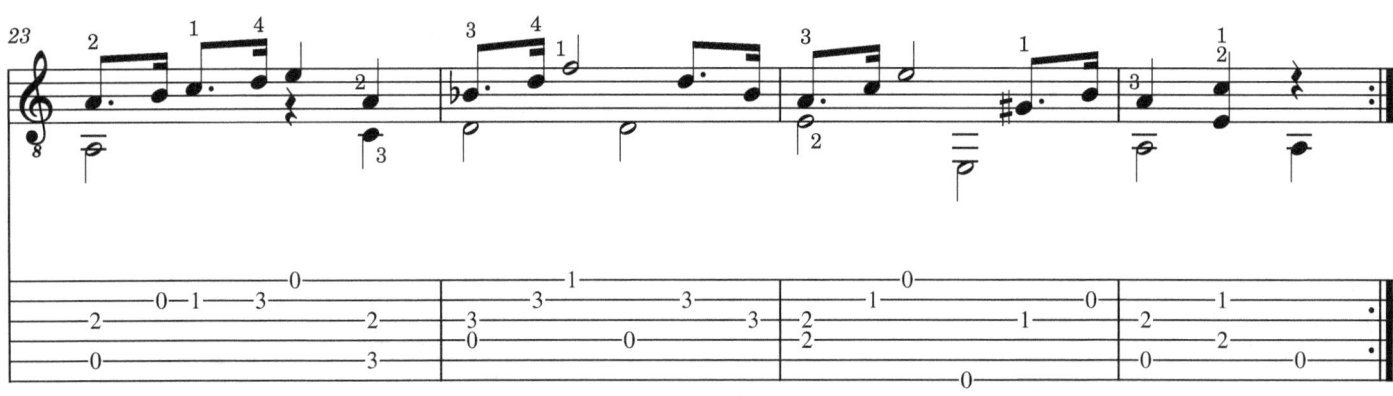

57

Pasa-Calle

José Viñas (1823-1888)

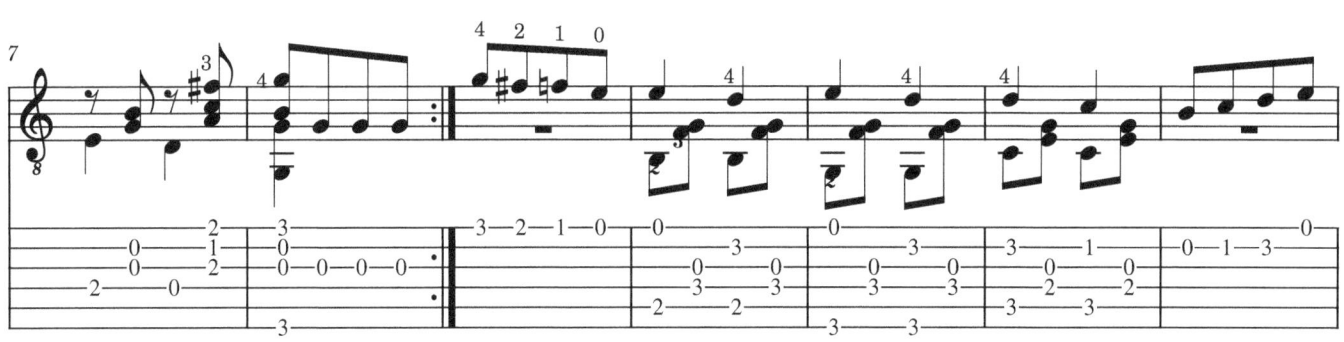

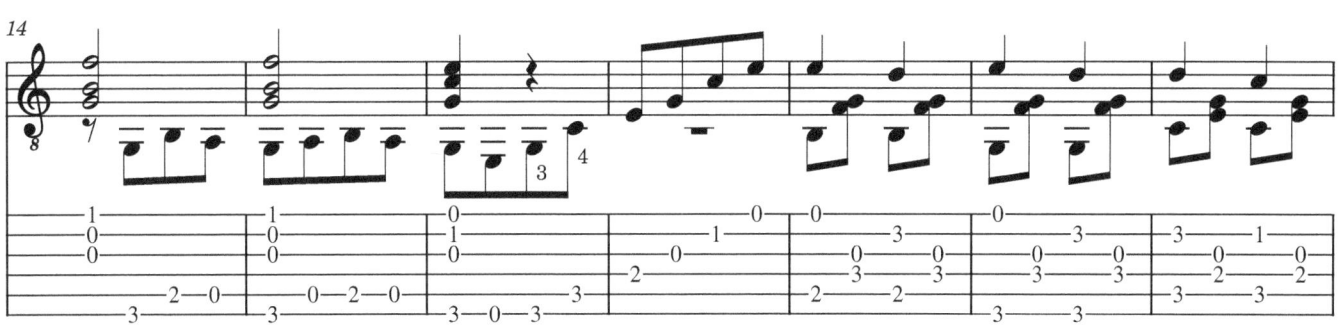

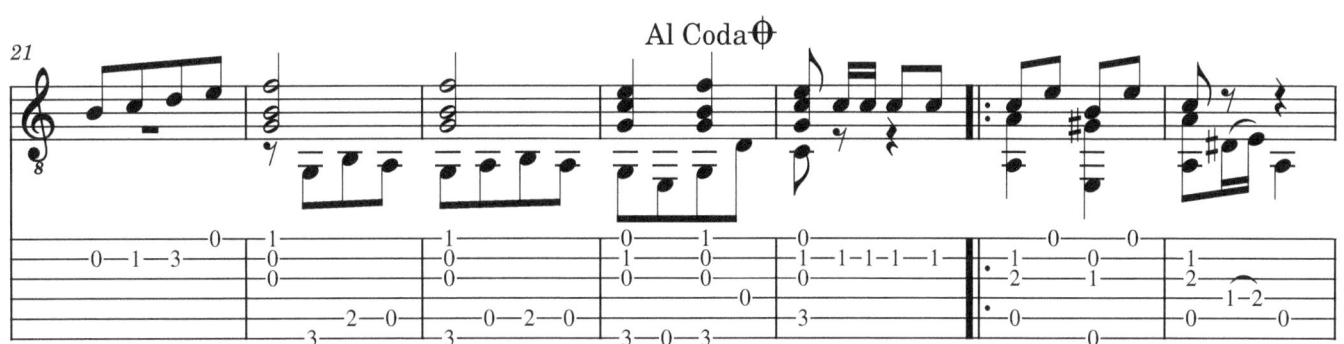

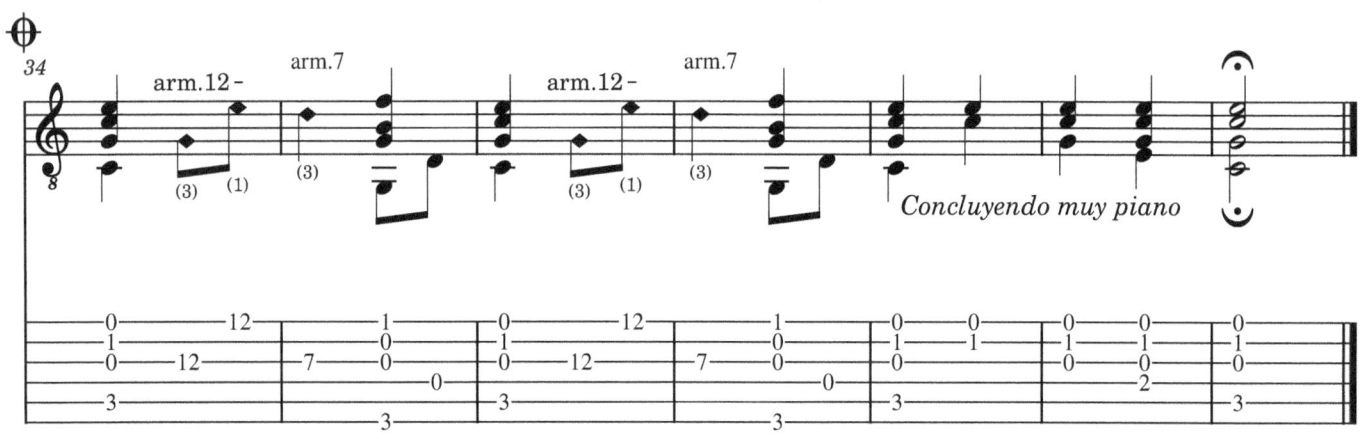

Polka

José Viñas (1823-1888)

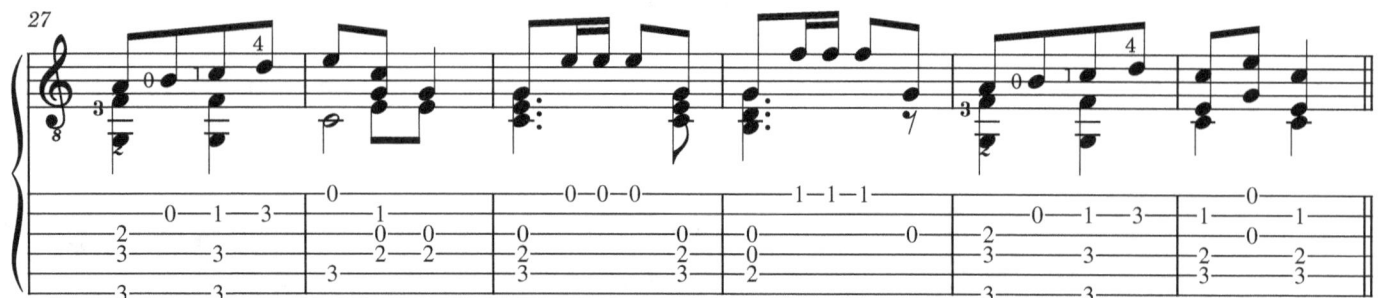

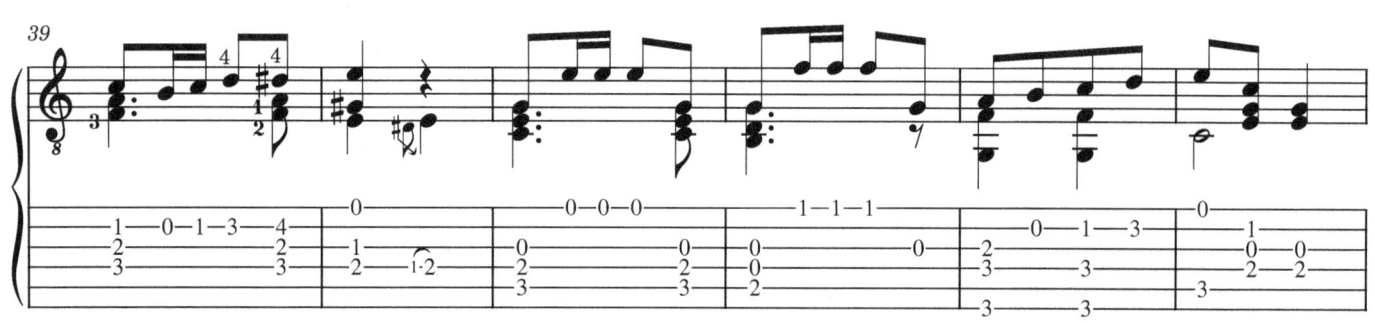

Vals

José Viñas (1823-1888)

Waltz

Napoleon Coste (1805 - 1883)

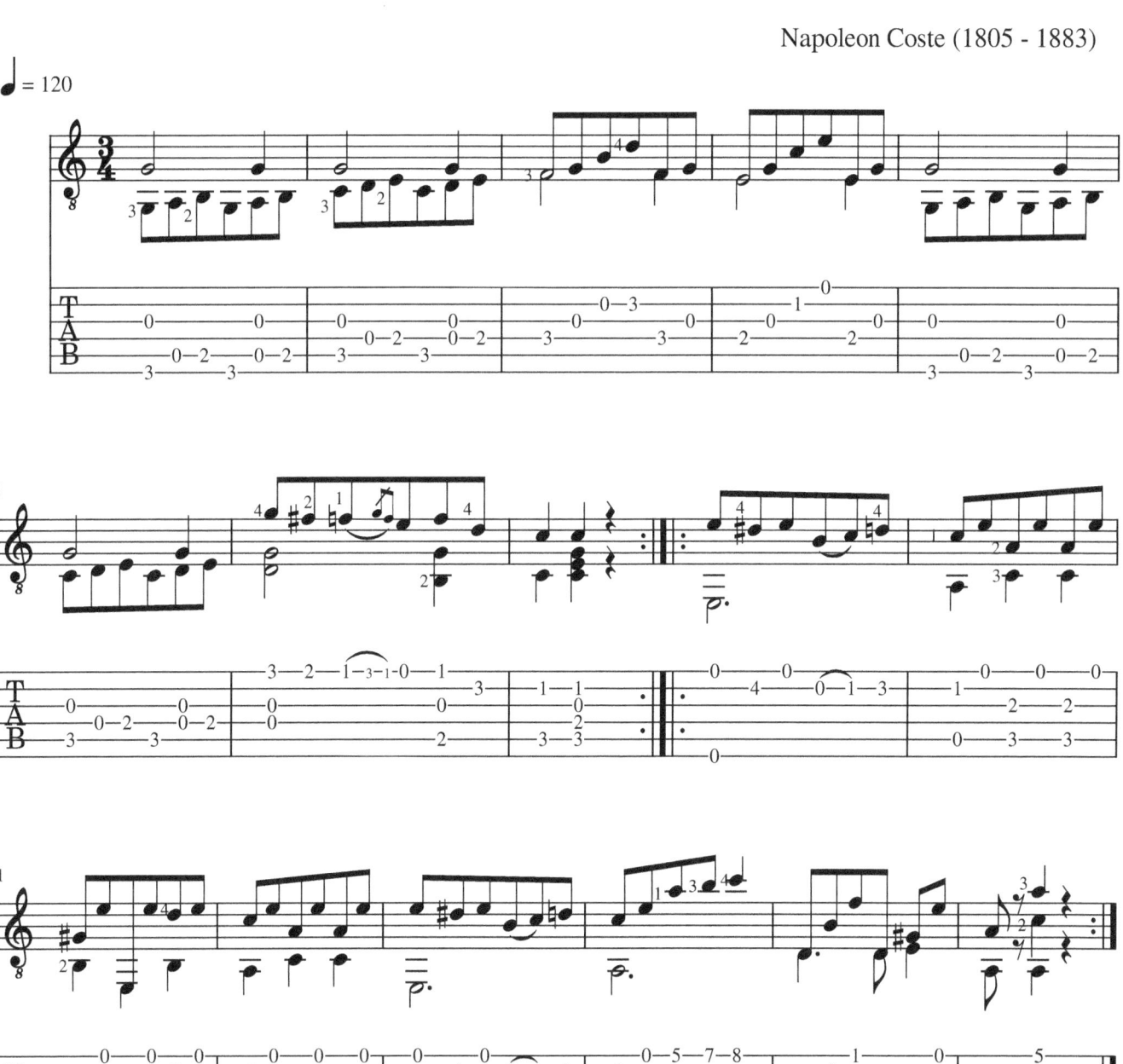

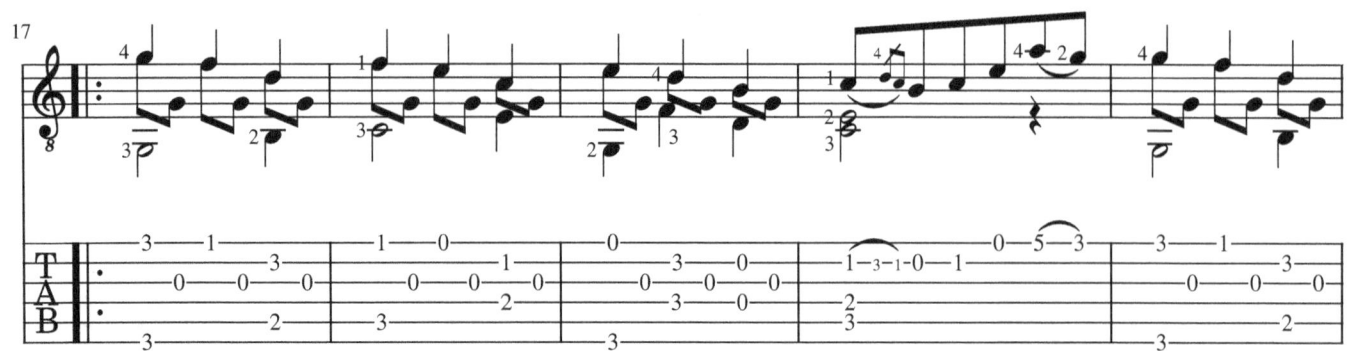

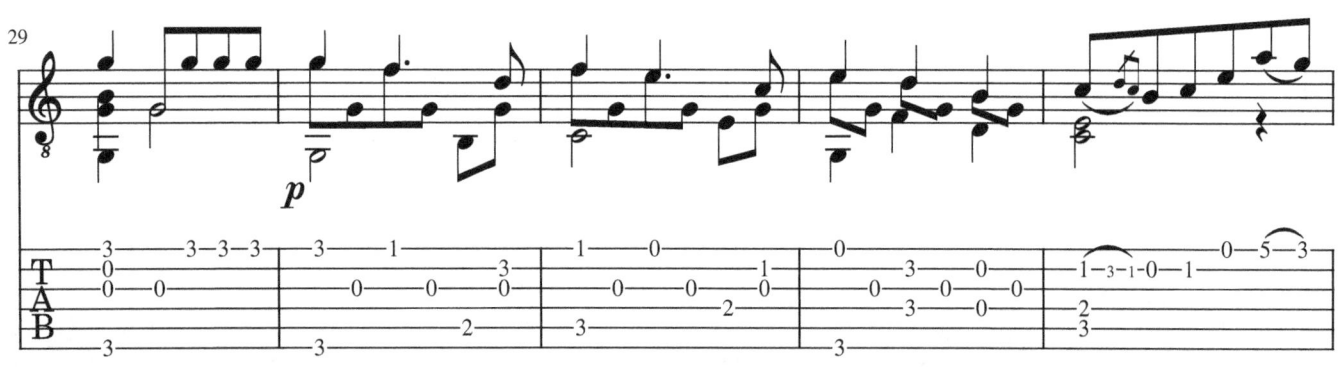
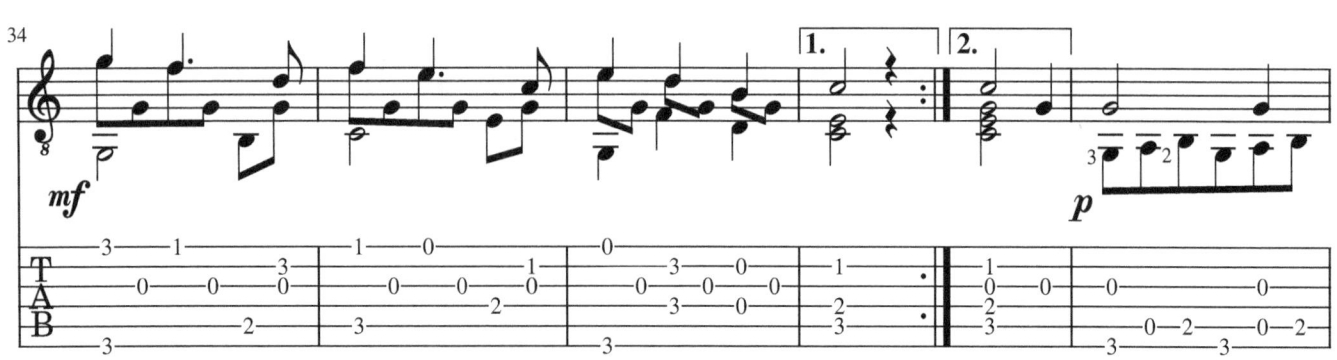

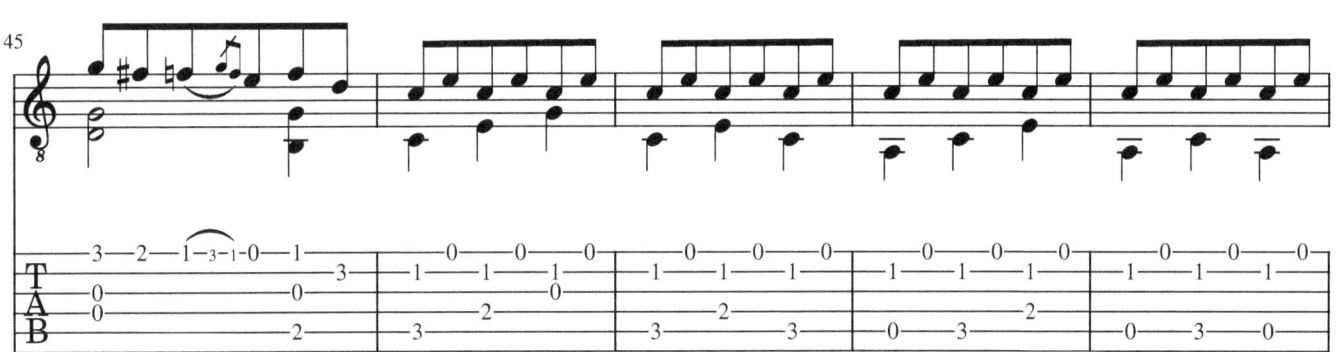

I lost my Eurydice

(Orphée) Gluck

Arr. Napoléon Coste (1805 - 1883)

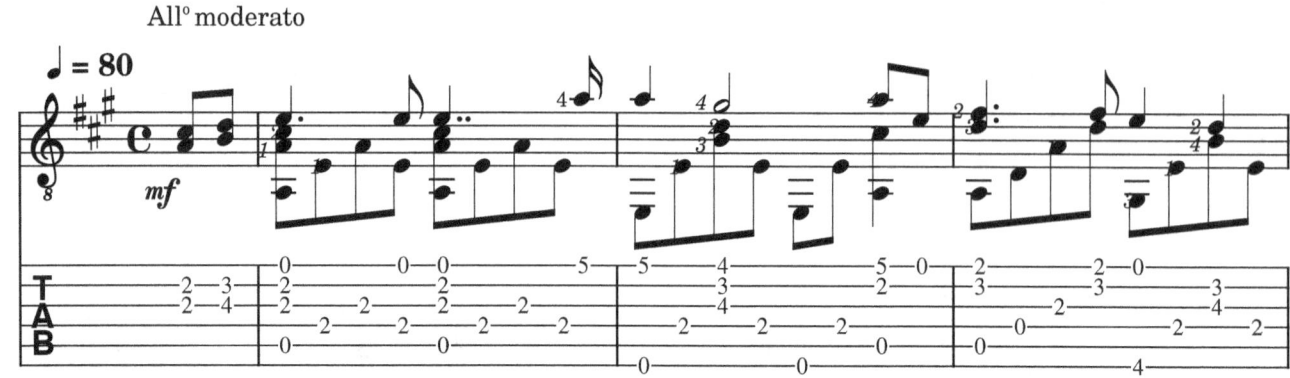

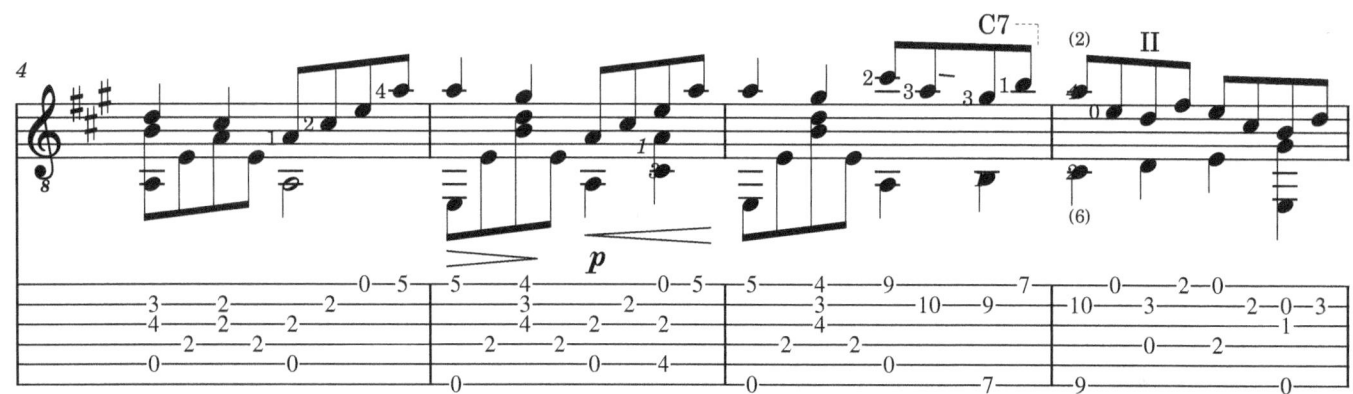

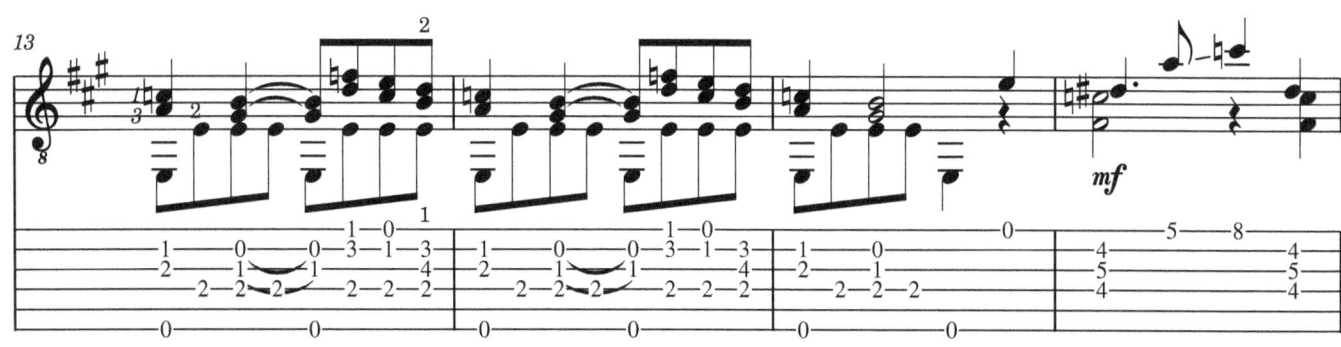

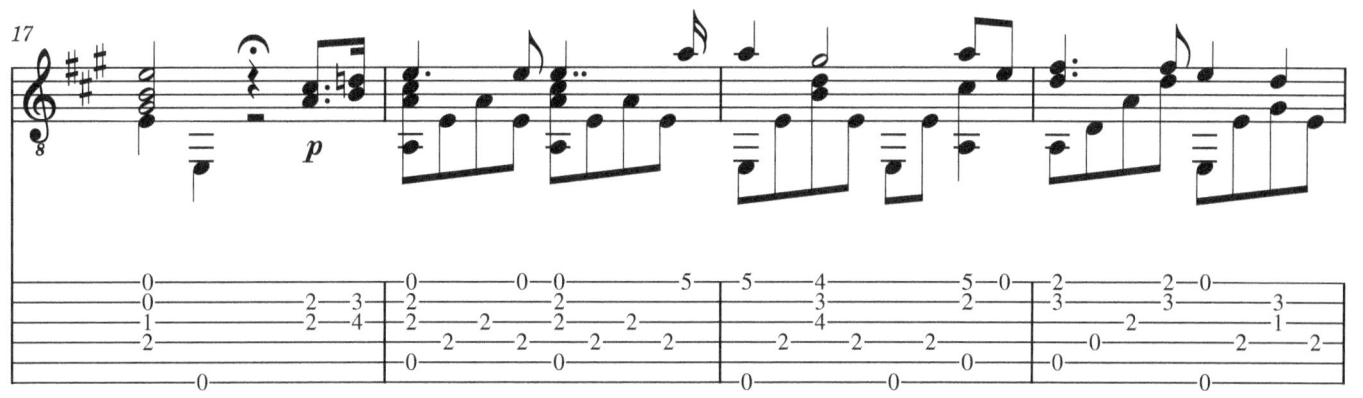
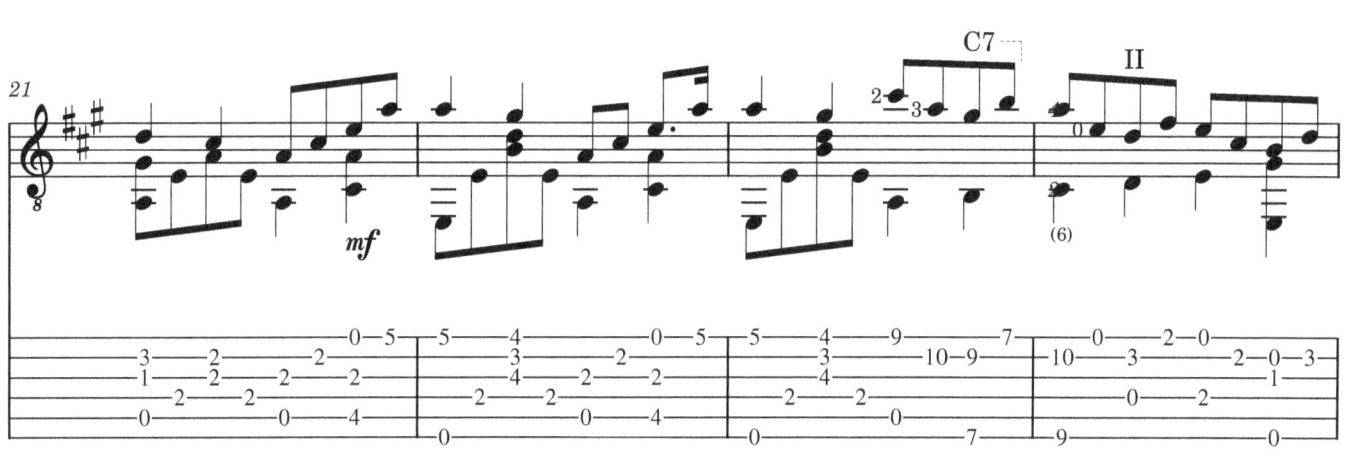
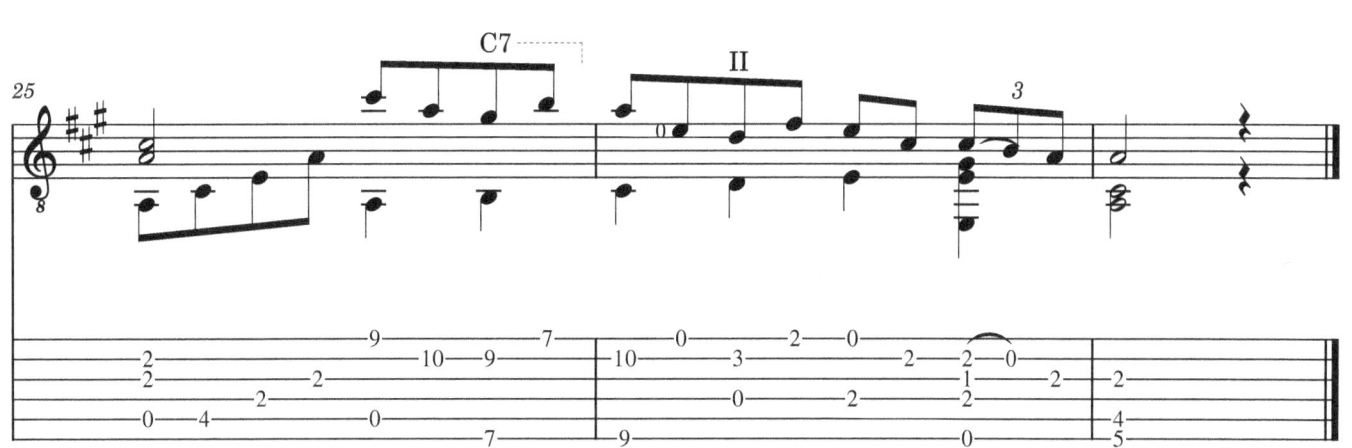

Barcarolle

Napoleon Coste (1805 - 1883)

Etude No.13

Napoleon Coste (1806 - 1883)

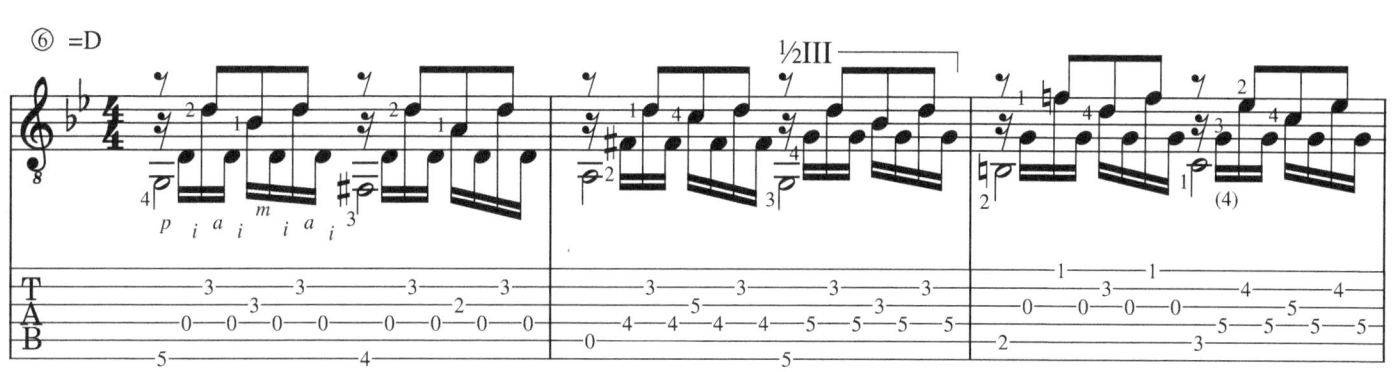

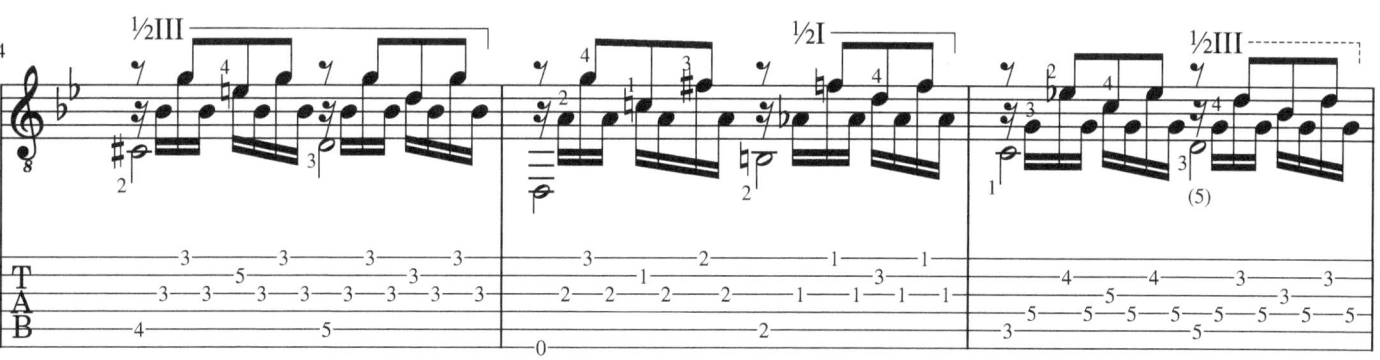

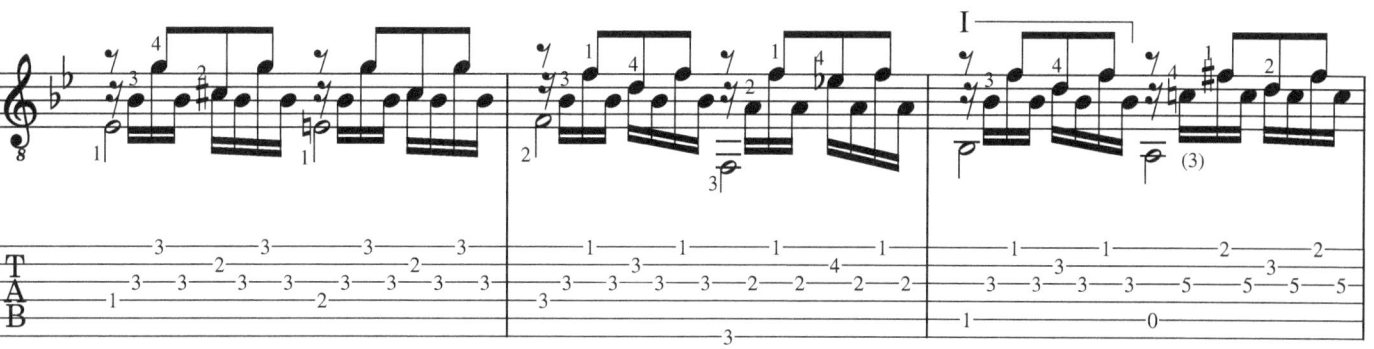

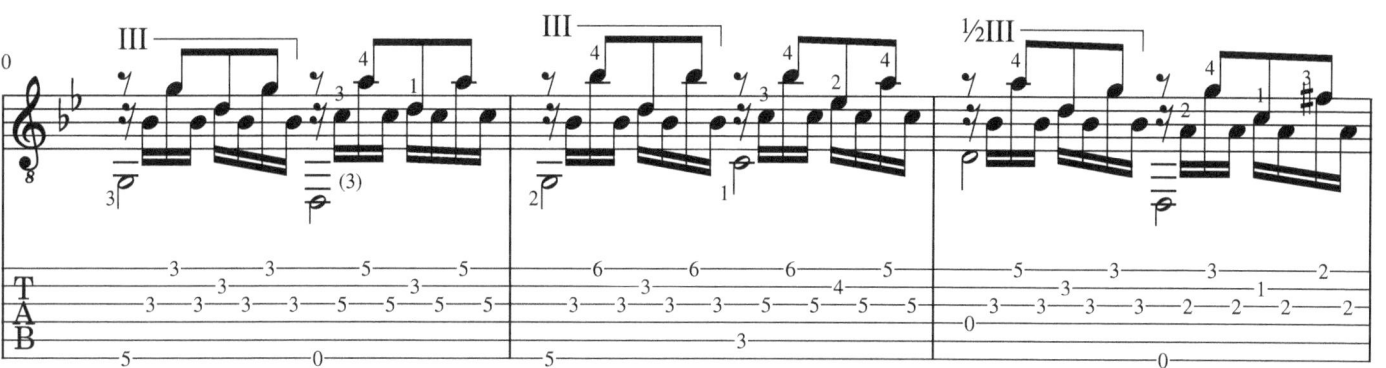

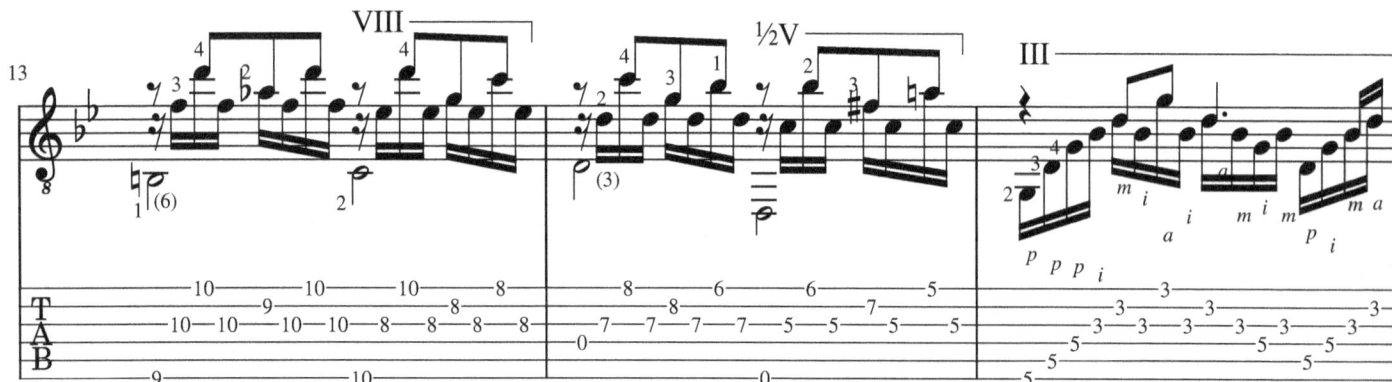

www.ingramcontent.com/pod-product-compliance
Lightning Source LLC
Chambersburg PA
CBHW080025080526
44585CB00018B/2118